AF344266

TOWARD ETHICAL PRACTICE

The Professional Practices in Adult Education and Human Resource Development Series explores issues and concerns of practitioners who work in the broad range of settings in adult and continuing education and human resource development.

The books are intended to provide information and strategies on how to make practice more effective for professionals and those they serve. They are written from a practical viewpoint and provide a forum for instructors, administrators, policy makers, counselors, trainers, managers, program and organizational developers, instructional designers, and other related professionals.

Michael W. Galbraith
Editor-in-Chief

TOWARD ETHICAL PRACTICE

Ralph G. Brockett
Roger Hiemstra

KRIEGER PUBLISHING COMPANY
MALABAR, FLORIDA
2004

Original Edition 2004

Printed and Published by
KRIEGER PUBLISHING COMPANY
KRIEGER DRIVE
MALABAR, FLORIDA 32950

Copyright © 2004 by Ralph G. Brockett and Roger Hiemstra

Library of Congress Cataloging-in-Publication Data

Brockett, Ralph Grover.
    Toward ethical practice / Ralph G. Brockett, Roger Hiemstra.
        p.   cm. — (Professional practices in adult education and human
        resource development series)
    Includes bibliographical references and index.
    ISBN 0-89464-993-0 (alk. paper)
    1. Teachers—Professional ethics. 2. Adult education. I. Hiemstra,
    Roger. II. Title. III. Series.
  LB1779.B76 2004
  174'.937—dc22   2003054618

10 9 8 7 6 5 4 3 2

CONTENTS

Preface — vii

Acknowledgments — xi

The Authors — xiii

1. What Is Ethical Practice? — 1

2. A Model for Ethical Decision Making — 13

3. Ethical Issues in Practice — 32

4. Common Concerns: Five Ethical Dilemmas — 52

5. Responding to Ethical Dilemmas — 70

6. Codes and Standards for Ethical Practice — 87

7. Creating an Ethical Environment — 98

8. Ethical Practice: Some Concluding Thoughts — 113

Appendix: A Workshop on Creating a Statement of Personal Philosophy — 121

References — 131

Index — 147

PREFACE

Ethics. Few words in the English language are likely to be more provocative. Ethics is about doing the right thing. But what is right in any given situation? Are we to view what is ethical as that which produces the greatest good for the most people? Are there universal standards that should be followed, regardless of the consequences of doing so? Or is ethics a relative term, where what is right depends on the setting or context in which behavior takes place? For centuries, questions such as these have guided the work of philosophers, and the answers continue to spark debate and controversy.

Today, ethics often conjures up an ominous feeling associated with scandal and wrongdoing in government, business, medicine, journalism, science, and nearly every other facet of modern life. How strange this seems, given that the term *ethics* centers on notions of what is good and on doing what is right.

In recent years, ethics has taken center stage in nearly all fields of professional practice. This emphasis seems to have intensified in the three decades since Watergate, and is reflected in a growing movement toward addressing rights and responsibilities of consumers and service providers. While some have attributed the surge of interest in ethics to a general breakdown in our society, others simply argue that ethics is a central element of professional practice and that the current emphasis on this area is a response to a need that has largely been ignored.

The point here is that ethics and ethical decision making are important because of the amount of power that professionals wield. Quite simply, where there is power, there is the potential—intentional or not—for abuse or misuse of that power. Although there are certainly situations where a professional may engage in behavior deemed questionable or inappropriate by others, it can be argued that in the vast majority of instances, unethical behavior is not so much the result of deliberate misconduct as unintentional misunderstanding or lack of awareness.

In *Toward Ethical Practice*, our purpose is to focus on ethical issues relative to one area of professional practice—working with adult learners. As is the case with many other professional fields, ethics has received relatively little attention in adult education and training. Yet, as with other professional fields, ethical dilemmas are part of the daily landscape of practice. Whether engaged in program development, administration, teaching, or advising, the educator or trainer who works with adults is continuously challenged by potential ethical dilemmas. By developing an understanding of ethical practice and strategies that can be used in ethical decision making, the educator or trainer is in a position to more effectively serve adult learners.

This book is intended for three main audiences. First, it is directed to educators and trainers who work in the many diverse settings where adult learners are served. We present illustrations of ethical dilemmas from such areas as business and industry, continuing professional education, adult basic education, higher education, and community-based programs. Second, it is targeted to graduate students in masters and doctoral degree programs in adult education and training. Our hope here is that the book can be used in a way that will infuse discussion of ethics and ethical decision making throughout the curriculum, as well as serve as a supplemental text in a wide range of courses. Third, while the focus of the book is on adult education and training, we believe that the model we present can be of use to readers from a wide range of settings. Just as our ideas have been informed by discussions of ethics from other fields, so too, we believe that our book may be useful to readers looking for a discussion of issues related to ethical decision making.

Toward Ethical Practice is not intended to provide you with prescriptive answers to specific ethical dilemmas you may face in your own practice. Rather, the book is intended to serve as a tool that can help you to (1) recognize potential ethical dilemmas that may arise in your practice, (2) raise questions that you can use to negotiate your way through ethical dilemmas you may experience, and (3) identify some strategies for demystifying and destigmatizing ethics in a way that can promote an environment where ethics is discussed in an open, non-confrontational manner. We do this by describing a *process* of ethical decision making rather than *prescriptive* solutions to specific ethical questions or problems.

The book opens by looking at the nature of ethical practice. Ethics is defined and described briefly. We follow this with the story of how the two of us became involved in studying and teaching about ethics as well as a review of some current developments from the literature on ethics in the education and training of adults.

In Chapter 2, we present the ethical decision-making (EDM) model. This process is the result of work that began nearly two decades ago and has evolved in large part as we had the opportunity to share our ideas with students and participants at conferences and workshops. The model serves as the framework for the book and centers on asking several key questions related to personal values, obligations, and the consequences of various options to addressing a dilemma.

Emphasis in the next two chapters shifts to an exploration of various dilemmas that can arise in practice. Chapter 3, "Ethical Issues in Practice," begins by expanding on the notion of values introduced in the previous chapter by discussing the development of a personal philosophy of education or training. Emphasis then shifts to discussion of ethical issues in the areas of teaching, training, planning, and implementing.

Chapter 4 continues the discussion of ethical dilemmas in practice by looking at what we have identified as common concerns—issues that have often been controversial in adult education and training and for which the potential for ethical conflict exists. From many possible issues, we selected five concerns to illustrate the possibilities: advocacy for social change, technology, censorship, marketing, and self-directed learning. For each common concern, we use the model described in Chapter 2 to analyze potential dilemmas.

Chapter 5 explores ways of responding to ethical dilemmas. Here, we present a worksheet that you can use to identify options and potential consequences when making ethical decisions. We also consider several responses to ethical dilemmas.

The question of whether adult education and training should develop and emphasize formal codes of ethics has been a source of considerable controversy in recent years. Chapter 6 focuses on this debate, offers examples of several current codes, and describes the types of ethical issues addressed by such codes.

While formal codes can have value in articulating common core values and desired practices, we believe that ultimately ethical practice is best facilitated through efforts to create an environment where ethics is used in a nonconfrontational way, rather than as a moral nightstick to promote fear and mistrust within an agency, program, or organization. In Chapter 7, we discuss a host of strategies that can be used to establish such an environment.

Finally, we revisit the main ideas and identify some tips that you should find useful as you think about your own ethical decision making. We also speculate about future directions for research relative to ethics in the education and training of adults.

ACKNOWLEDGMENTS

We are grateful to many people who have helped us throughout the extended period of time it has taken us to complete this book. First, we would like to thank Michael Galbraith, series editor, who believed in this project from the outset and offered valuable suggestions as we conceptualized the book. Mary Roberts, senior editor at Krieger, has been a tremendous support and is a wonderful editor. We are especially grateful to our spouses, Mary Rowden Brockett and Janet Hiemstra, for their love and support. Finally, we wish to acknowledge the many graduate students, workshop participants, and conference attendees who, by their examples and shared situations, have helped us bring abstract ideas to life.

THE AUTHORS

Ralph G. Brockett is Professor and Coordinator, Adult Education, the University of Tennessee, Knoxville. He holds a B.A. in psychology and an M.Ed. in guidance and counseling from the University of Toledo. He also holds a Ph.D. in adult education from Syracuse University where he focused his doctoral research on self-directed learning and was involved with an innovative weekend scholar masters in adult education program.

Previously, he held faculty positions at Montana State University and Syracuse University and has worked in continuing education program development for health and human service professionals. He is a past chair of the Commission of Professors of Adult Education and board member of the American Association for Adult and Continuing Education. In addition, he is coeditor of *Adult Learning* and has held positions on the editorial boards of three adult education journals and previously was editor-in-chief of *New Directions for Adult and Continuing Education*.

His books include *The Power and Potential of Collaborative Partnerships* (1998, coedited with I. M. Saltiel and A. Sgori); *The Profession and Practice of Adult Education* (1997, with S. B. Merriam and winner of Houle Award for Outstanding Literature in Adult Education); *Overcoming Resistance to Self-Direction in Adult Learning* (1994, coedited with R. Hiemstra); *Self-Direction in Adult Learning: Perspectives on Theory, Research, and Practice* (1991, with R. Hiemstra); *Professional Development for Educators of Adults* (1991); *Ethical Issues in Adult Education* (1988, editor and chapter contributor); *Adult and Continuing Education* (1988, coedited with S. E. Easton and J. O. Picton); and *Continuing Education in the Year 2000* (1987).

Brockett's major scholarly interests are in the areas of professional ethics in adult education, self-direction in adult learning, and the study of the field of adult education.

Roger Hiemstra is Professor and Chair, Adult Education, Elmira College. He received his B.S. degree in agricultural economics from Michigan State University, his M.S. degree in extension education from Iowa State University, and his Ph.D. degree in adult community education from the University of Michigan. He was a Mott Intern in the community education program in Flint, Michigan.

Hiemstra served as county extension agent for the Iowa Cooperative Extension Service, where he first began working with adults as learners. He then taught adult education at the University of Nebraska. He has since served as professor and department chair of adult education at Iowa State University and Syracuse University and is Professor Emeritus at Syracuse University. Hiemstra was inducted into the International Adult and Continuing Education Hall of Fame in 2000.

His books include another in the Professional Practices Series, *Professional Writing: Processes, Strategies, and Tips for Publishing in Educational Journals* (1994, with E. M. Brier); *Overcoming Resistance to Self-Direction in Adult Learning* (1994, coedited with R. G. Brockett); *Self-Direction in Adult Learning: Perspectives on Theory, Research, and Practice* (1991, with R. G. Brockett); *Environments for Effective Adult Learning* (1991, editor and chapter contributor); *Individualizing Instruction: Making Learning Personal, Empowering, and Successful* (1990, with B. R. Sisco); *Lifelong Learning* (1976); and *The Educative Community* (1972).

He has also served as editor of *Lifelong Learning: The Adult Years* and of the *Adult Education Quarterly* and was chair of the Commission of Professors of Adult Education. His major scholarly interests are on the use of technology to create opportunities for adult learners, including distance learning, teaching on-line courses, and the training of trainers in using web-based technology; the identification of teaching and training implications and resources related to adult, self-directed learning; and discovering ways educators can utilize community resources and technology to promote learning.

CHAPTER 1

What Is Ethical Practice?

On June 17, 1972, five men broke into an office building in Washington, D.C. What at first appeared to be a simple burglary produced a chain of events that ultimately led to the resignation of a United States president. It also set in motion a whole new way of thinking about the moral responsibilities of those who hold positions of power.

Today, everywhere we turn we hear talk of ethics. In politics, terms like Abscam, Iran Contra, and Whitewater conjure up images of the post-Watergate era, and numerous political careers have ended or been seriously affected by "scandals" that, before Watergate, would likely have gone unnoticed. Indeed, the 1999 impeachment of President Bill Clinton and the controversies surrounding the 2000 presidential election will likely keep ethics at the forefront of national politics for years to come.

Ethical concerns are not limited to the political arena. In the health professions, medical ethics has long been an area of focus; most recently, issues such as abortion and assisted suicide have seriously divided the public. Similarly, the sciences regularly grapple with ethical questions, such as those surrounding cloning or the human genome.

The business world has also been a focal point for discussions of ethics. The year 2002 saw unethical behaviors by leaders in such companies as Adelphia, Arthur Andersen, Enron, and WorldCom that led to personal and financial pain and heartbreak for many people. Indeed, many companies have gone as far as to institute "ethics training" programs for their employees.

Religious leaders, too, have come under attack in terms of ethical, moral, and even criminal behavior. The 1980s saw the demise of evangelist Jim Baker for various kinds of questionable behavior. During the ensuing years, several ministers or church leaders were involved with financial misdeeds or immoral behavior of varying types. The beginning of the 21st century has seen numerous Catholic priests accused of child molestation, with accompanying suggestions that the church hierarchy may have been involved in cover-up efforts.

Finally, the field of journalism has especially become a lightning rod for those who are concerned with questions of ethics. Several years ago, when tennis star Arthur Ashe held a press conference to reveal that he had AIDS, he did so only because a reporter was about to reveal it in a newspaper story. And one need only think of the O. J. Simpson murder trial and the tragic circumstances surrounding the death of Princess Diana and her companions to understand how central ethical practice is in the world of news reporting.

What do these examples have to do with adult education or training? Perhaps nowhere in contemporary society is the concern over ethics more visible than within the professions. Historically, professionals generally have been highly regarded by society at large. Because their training and knowledge qualify them to provide specialized services, professionals have been looked upon as respected authorities in their area of practice.

In more recent times, however, this functionalist view of professions and professionals has come under attack. Today, as the emphasis on consumer activism is rising, many critics charge that professions are characterized by elitism and that many professionals are overly concerned with cornering and controlling services and knowledge (Cervero, 1988). A discussion of what is sometimes viewed as a crisis in the professions is beyond the scope of our discussion here; however, it is important to note that much of the concern regarding professional ethics has arisen due to charges of elitism, incompetence, and even abuse.

Quite simply, then, ethics is important to adult educators and trainers because of the power that professionals wield. The decisions professionals make and the actions they take can have tremendous, even life and death, implications for the clients they serve. While most professionals are committed to providing their services with care and integrity, the reality remains that there is the potential for abuse or misuse of power, whether unintentional or by design.

Thus, although its content has wider application, this book focuses primarily on ethics and ethical practice in relation to a specific area of activity: the education and training of adults. While there is much debate over whether adult education and training meet the definition of a profession, what is clear is that those of us who work with adult learners deal with specific kinds of professional services. And while we rarely find ourselves in "life and death" or geographically broad impact situations, the decisions we make do have an impact on the lives of those whom we serve. The way in which we approach learners can have a tremendous impact on their ultimate success or failure.

To illustrate this point, think about how so many adults who seek out opportunities for education and training do so with a degree of fear, doubt, or insecurity. For example, those individuals who enroll in a literacy program are often saddled with a fear of failure or painful memories of their past schooling experiences. In a study of migrant adults enrolled in a general education development (GED) program, Velázquez (1993) found that while most participants valued learning, they described their previous experiences with education and schooling as painful and meaningless. Likewise, adults who seek to enroll in higher education institutions may find themselves asking: "Have I been away from school too long to be able to do this again?" "How will I balance my job and family responsibilities with going to college?" "Can I really learn this?" Adults who participate in workplace training programs may face similar apprehensions. They also may have concerns about the relevance of learning to their current or future job performance.

As educators of adults we have a very real opportunity to make differences in the lives of others. But we are also in a power position where our words and actions can intimidate, discourage, disempower, and even dissuade those with whom we come in contact. We have all heard stories about an advisor or guidance counselor telling potential students that they were "not college material" (it happened to Ralph during his senior year of high school and to Roger even while in college). For some, this kind of comment can provide motivation to succeed in order to "prove them wrong." But for others, it is a proverbial kiss of death that can lead to a self-fulfilling hopelessness feeling or even choosing not to try.

And what about the teacher or trainer who intimidates or verbally abuses students in the belief that this will help to toughen them? Or the college administrator who recommends closing a Reentry Student Office because of a belief that special programs can separate and alienate certain groups of students? Such actions, of course, are not necessarily deliberate attempts to undermine the efforts of adult learners. For example, an advisor may believe that some personal assessment, though negative, is honest and open and thus in the best interest of the student. Nonetheless these examples illustrate how ethical concerns or dilemmas can arise in daily decision making.

There are rarely easy answers to ethical dilemmas found in daily practice. However, in this book, we will help you find answers by providing tools and ideas that you can use in your own practice. We begin by briefly defining ethics and related concepts. The emphasis then shifts to a look at how ethics and ethical practice have been viewed to date within the context of adult education and training.

WHAT IS ETHICS?

A good place to begin our journey is to ask a seemingly simple question: What is ethics? Most of us have an image that comes to mind when we hear the word *ethics*; yet, if asked, we might have a difficult time coming up with a clear, simple definition.

Kidder (1995) states that ethics is "about the inner impulses, judgements, and duties of people like you and me" (p. 63). Fagothey (1972) has defined ethics as "the study of right and wrong, of good and evil, in human conduct" (p. 2). Frankena (1973) defines ethics as a branch of moral philosophy involving "philosophical thinking about morality, moral problems, and moral judgements" (p. 4). Finally, MacKinnon (2001) also describes ethics as moral philosophy and points out that ethics "asks basic questions about the good life, about what is better and worse, about whether there is any objective right and wrong, and how we know if there is" (p. 4).

What can we glean from these definitions? First, ethics is closely aligned with morality and moral behavior. Pojman (1995) makes some distinctions by using "morality to refer to certain customs, precepts, and practices of people and cultures . . . moral philosophy to refer to philosophical or theoretical reflection on morality . . . [and] ethics to refer to the whole domain of morality and moral philosophy" (p. 2). Similarly, Thiroux (1986) notes that ethics "seems to pertain to the individual character of a person or persons, whereas morality seems to point to the relationships among human beings" (p. 2).

On the other hand, Kidder (1995) argues: "There is little to be gained by trying to distinguish rigidly between morals and ethics. Some think of the former as personal and the latter as institutional" (p. 64). He goes on to say that some people see morals as "restricted to sexual matters" while ethics covers "all other right-and-wrong matters" (p. 64). In this book, we use the two terms interchangeably while recognizing that there may be subtle differences between them.

Second, it is important to recognize that the term *ethics* can have several different, though related, meanings. Thompson (2000) makes this point by distinguishing between three forms of ethics, each of which has a different meaning. Descriptive ethics is the most straightforward form. According to Thompson, this approach to ethics centers on a "description of the way in which people live, and the moral choices they make" (2000, p. 29). It is based on stating facts that may or may not be accurate. For example, take the statement, "during any given year, most adults participate in some form of learning." For those of us committed to working with adult learners, and who believe in the importance of adult education, it is easy to agree with this statement. However, such agreement does not take into consideration the statement's accuracy, nor does it make any inferences about whether what was learned is good or bad.

A second form is typically referred to as metaethics. Metaethics involves the formal study of ethics, and usually is the work of philosophers or others with specialized background in philosophical inquiry. According to Thompson, metaethics is "not concerned with the content of moral discourse, but with its meaning" (p. 31). The earlier definition of ethics by Fagothey (1972) is an example of metaethics because it focuses on the study of good and bad or right and wrong, not the real-life instances of such behavior.

A third way of understanding ethics is often referred to as normative ethics. Normative ethics, according to Thompson, "is concerned with ideas about what is right, about justice, about how people should live. It examines the choices people make and the values and reasoning that lie behind them" (2000, p. 20). Basically, normative ethics is where judgments about values in a particular moral issue are addressed.

Thus, to summarize, descriptive ethics centers on facts or "what is," metaethics involves the academic study of ethics, and normative ethics emphasizes values or questions of "what ought to be" (Thompson, 2000). While these perspectives are interrelated, and each can be relevant to ethical practice, in this book we focus on normative ethics.

In thinking through our approach, we believe that it is not enough to simply describe situations as they exist. This, in and of itself, will not contribute to ethical practice. Similarly, because metaethics involves the academic study of theories and concepts in ethics, this emphasis is beyond the everyday world of most people involved in the education and training of adults. On the other hand, the normative approach has practical appeal because it emphasizes the application of ethics to practical situations. In other words, you do not need to be an ethicist in order to be concerned with ethical practice.

This does not mean that we eschew ethics as a topic of academic study. To the contrary, the extent to which we extend our understanding of applied, professional ethics will largely be determined by the kinds of discourse that take place among academic ethicists. Both of us, for example, teach graduate courses that deal in some way with the study of ethics and ethical behaviors. However, we reemphasize our normative ethics assumption that you do not need formal training in ethics to reflect and act on ethical dilemmas that arise in practice.

ETHICS IN ADULT EDUCATION AND TRAINING

While ethics has emerged as a truly hot topic within many professions and in society at large, its development in adult education and training literature has been somewhat slower. In this section, we highlight some related developments relative to ethics. We begin by sharing our own stories on how we came to write this book. Then we conclude by describing where the literature has contributed to our current understanding of ethics.

On the Road to Ethical Practice: A Personal Journey

This anecdotal material is designed to provide some insight into the perspective from which we have written this book. It also reinforces our notion that the ethics of practice should not be left only to those whose formal academic preparation has been in this area. Rather than either of us being an ethicist who is interested in adult education and training, each of us is a professional educator of adults with an interest in ethical practice.

How did we become involved with ethics in the education and training of adults? For Roger, the journey began in 1970 when he joined the University of Nebraska faculty. Over the years, at Nebraska and later at Iowa State and Syracuse Universities, Roger regularly taught a program planning and evaluation course. In discussing issues relative to program planning, ethics seemed to emerge as an important area. Roger accumulated a small collection of writings on ethics, drawn mostly from the social intervention litera-

ture (for example, Warwick & Kelman, 1976), to help students think through ethical decisions on various program planning issues.

In 1982, Ralph joined Roger on the Syracuse University faculty. During our first semester as faculty colleagues, we co-taught the program planning and evaluation course. When doing an assessment of class members' learning needs and interests, we were not surprised to see that ethics ranked high. Ralph took the lead on this topic using Roger's collection of related articles as a starting point. He next searched the adult education literature for additional material, but only a few resources surfaced. Only one, a study of ethical practice among training professionals, was based on empirical data (Clement, Pinto, & Walker, 1978). Ralph used these resources in leading related class discussion. Another key article (Singarella & Sork, 1983) was published a year later and used in subsequent program planning courses.

A little later, shortly after moving to Montana State University, Ralph was approached about doing an edited book of original chapters on adult education ethics. He was interested in the opportunity, but the initial publisher decided not to pursue the topic. Still believing that there was a need for broad discussion on the topic, Ralph discussed the notion with several colleagues and subsequently approached another publisher with a book idea. Eventually, a contract was awarded, the work completed, and the book published in 1988.

The intent of this book, *Ethical Issues in Adult Education* (Brockett, 1988a), was to create an awareness of ethical issues that can arise in adult education practice and to help readers think further about these issues. What still remains in Ralph's view as the true accomplishment of this effort is the willingness of prominent scholars in the adult education field to be a part of the project. The chapter authors included the following: Ralph Brockett, Stephen Brookfield, John Burns, Rosemary Caffarella, Robert Carlson, Phyllis Cunningham, Michael Day,

Roger Hiemstra, Carol Kasworm, Sharan Merriam, Gene Roche, Burton Sisco, and Thomas Sork.

Once the book was published, Ralph had the opportunity to make several presentations on ethics and incorporated ethics content into different courses. One such presentation was subsequently turned into an article (Brockett, 1991). For Roger, his chapter on developing a personal philosophy was an opportunity to pull together ideas that he had used in his teaching for many years (Hiemstra, 1988). Both of us continue to use this chapter today in helping students develop personal philosophy statements in various adult education courses. More recently, the two of us collaborated to develop a graduate course on ethics and adult education that was first offered at Elmira College by Ralph in the summer of 1999, and subsequently by Roger in 2001. See Hiemstra (2002) to examine the course syllabus.

Current Developments

The original purpose of *Ethical Issues in Adult Education* was to stimulate interest in and dialogue and further writing about the topic. In the years since 1988 the literature on ethics in adult education and training has begun to grow. A number of articles and conference papers have explored ethics and at least two books have focused on aspects of ethics in adult education.

For example, the question of a code of ethics for adult education and training has been debated at some length. Those who argue for such a code (Connelly & Light, 1991; Griffith, 1991; Siegel, 2000; Sork & Welock, 1992; Wood, 1996) discuss the need for ways to ensure consumer protection, self-regulation, and a framework to guide ethical practice. In the area of human resource development, Hatcher and Aragon (2000a, 2000b) discuss a rationale for the development of the *Standards on Ethics and Integrity* of the Academy of Human Resource Development. Lawler (2000) surveyed members of the Association for Continuing Higher Education (ACHE); the result of this survey was the development of a code for the ACHE.

On the other hand, critics of such codes (Carlson, 1988; Collins, 1991; Cunningham, 1992) argue that formal codes are not feasible because the field is too diverse to be guided by a single set of standards. Also, according to critics, codes are not desirable because they serve to promote elitism as they "privilege a group of persons who either are in or working toward gaining positions of power" (Cunningham, 1992, p. 107).

Although research on ethics to date has been limited, there have been a few such investigations. For example, two studies have looked at how adult education practitioners view ethical issues and codes of ethics. McDonald and Wood (1993) surveyed a group of adult educators and trainers in Indiana. Of the 249 respondents, 30% identified examples of ethical dilemmas they had encountered in their practice. The most frequently identified dilemmas included confidentiality, ownership of instructional materials, employment practices, conflicts of interest, and financial issues. Further, McDonald and Wood found that more than half of the respondents (52.2%) believed that there should be a code of ethics "for themselves and other adult educators" (1993, p. 249).

Gordon and Sork (2001) replicated this study with a sample of 261 respondents from British Columbia. In the Canadian study, it was found that the most frequently identified dilemmas were confidentiality, the learner–adult educator relationship, finance, professionalism and competence, conflicts of interest, and evaluation of student performance. As for the code of ethics question, 72.8% supported the need for such a code. Thus, the findings of the earlier study were, for the most part, supported.

To date, the majority of literature on ethics in adult education and training has focused on aspects of ethics as they relate to practice, such as Sork's Ethical Practices Analysis (1990), ethical development and implications for practice (Ellis & McElhinney, 1992, 1993), ethics and program planning (Brockett & Hiemstra, 1998), and a model for analyzing ethical problems (Lawler & Fielder, 1991).

At least three books have looked at ethical dimensions of adult education. Cervero and Wilson (1994), in a discussion of power issues in the program planning process, addressed ethics as a central element of their framework. Jarvis (1997) has offered a discussion of ethics in adult education grounded in existentialism. In this book, Jarvis looks at ethical aspects of such areas as learning, education and training distinctions, mentoring, self-directed and contract learning, distance education, assessment, and adult education as a social movement. Most recently, Hatcher (2002) has offered a look at ethics in the area of human resource development (HRD). This book revolves around the idea that HRD is at a point in time where it can "assume leadership in enhancing ethically and socially responsible organizations" (p. 16). In addition to a rationale and conceptual framework, the book addresses such topics as business ethics, social responsibility, globalization, technology, development and economics, and the enviromnent.

The above provides only a brief introduction to the available literature. Subsequent chapters describe how the literature has impacted adult education and training in various ways.

THE NEED FOR THIS BOOK

Returning for a moment to our personal anecdote, as more authors added their insights to the literature and as we gave presentations at conferences, workshops, and our graduate classes, it seemed as if there were a need to take the discussion of ethics further. Ralph began to rethink the decision-making framework he presented in the 1988 book's opening chapter. He approached Roger about the idea of coauthoring a new book on ethics. In the meantime, Ralph and Roger wrote a chapter on ethics for a book on program planning (Brockett & Hiemstra, 1998). As sometimes happens, a host of personal and professional factors entered our lives and prolonged the completion of this book. However, we believe that this additional time allowed us to gain new insights and collect examples of ethical concerns that ultimately helped bring the book to life.

Our point in sharing our personal journeys is to show that ethics is a topic that "just happened" to both of us. Neither of us, at the beginning of our teaching careers, would have anticipated that we would be writing about this topic. However, with a combined five decades as professors, and the fact that our paths have led us to spend considerable time reflecting on ethical practice, we are at a time and place to present our collective ideas to others who are concerned with ethical decision making in adult education and training. We share the fruits of our journeys with you in the following chapters and look forward to much ensuing dialogue.

CHAPTER 2

A Model for Ethical Decision Making

In the previous chapter, we discussed how ethical dilemmas can permeate nearly every aspect of practice in adult education and training. While these dilemmas are sometimes a case of right versus wrong, more often they involve questions of right versus right. As Weston (1997) states, "we have an ethical issue precisely because we have conflicts between different things, perhaps incompatible things, that are good" (pp. 54–55). For example, Kidder (1995, p. 17) points out that "[i]t is right to extend equal social services to everyone regardless of race or ethnic origin—and right to pay special attention to those whose cultural backgrounds may have deprived them of past opportunities."

This point is relevant in the context of adult education and training. For instance, it may be "right" to view education as a vehicle to benefit a corporation or even society at large while simultaneously attending to the individual needs of learners. However, when it becomes necessary to make a choice between which of these directions should prevail, we can see an ethical dilemma in the making. Quite often, the dilemmas we face in our practice do not involve a deliberate, conscious effort by someone to act in an unethical way. Rather, they are borne out of conflicting values or obligations and often there is not a clear direction as to what is right.

Our basic premise throughout this book is that there are no easy solutions to most right versus right dilemmas and no simple prescriptive formula to tell us how to act in a specific situation. At the same time, we believe there are fundamental questions that educators and trainers of adults should ask them-

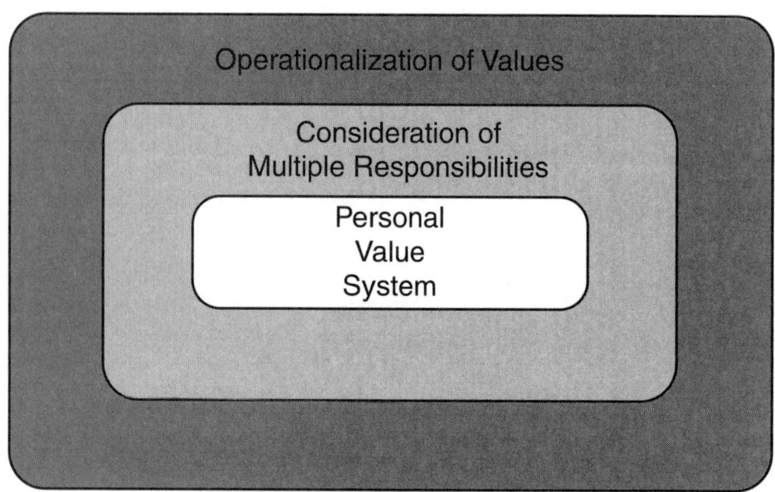

Figure 2.1 Dimensions of ethical practice in adult education (Brockett, 1988b)

selves when faced with a dilemma in their practice. In this chapter, we present a process designed to help educators become aware of several ethical decision-making components and to raise questions that can be useful in negotiating a way through such dilemmas.

In *Ethical Issues in Adult Education*, Brockett presents a model (see Figure 2.1) that differentiates among three dimensions of ethical practice (1988b). At its heart is the personal value system. These values form the beliefs that, consciously or unconsciously, educators carry with them in their practice. In addition, this dimension addresses the degree to which a person is committed to specific personal values. An educator or trainer deeply committed to certain values is more likely to fight for these rather than those much less central to that person's value system.

The second dimension refers to a consideration of multiple responsibilities. This dimension illustrates that the responsibilities of educators and trainers extend in many directions. For example, educators are simultaneously responsible to the learners they serve, their organization, their profession, society, and themselves to name a few. In reality, ethical dilemmas often arise "not because roles are unclear but because they are clearly in conflict" (Mirvits & Seashore, 1979, p. 771).

The third practice dimension refers to the operationalization of values. Here the focus is on how educators translate values into practice and discussion centers on an identification of both general guidelines and the code of ethics question.

The model was initially proposed to stimulate discussion and raise questions for understanding what encompasses ethical practice. However, it became clear that the initial model was only a starting point. Two concerns surfaced. First, while the model was presented as three levels with each successive level building on top of previous ones, it is actually a linear model because each dimension builds outward from the core in a stepwise sequence. The model therefore begins with the personal value system, then incorporates consideration of multiple responsibilities, and finally the operationalization of values. Second, some of the phrases used to describe the dimensions were unclear. Thus, we have refined the original model to better reflect our current understanding of ethical decision making.

A PROCESS FOR RESPONDING TO ETHICAL DILEMMAS

No simple, clear-cut steps exist to assure that a person acts ethically. Ethical decision making is complex and influenced by many factors. Thus, we present here a process we believe is helpful in making ethical decisions. The usefulness stems from guiding educators of adults to ask some basic questions about key aspects of ethical practice. The model for ethical decision making (EDM) and its related questions are illustrated in Figures 2.2 and 2.3.

Essentially, the EDM model is founded on the idea that in responding to an ethical dilemma, three elements need to be considered: (1) personal *values*; (2) an awareness of where *obligations* lie; and (3) an understanding of possible responses to a dilemma and the corresponding *consequences* of any decision.

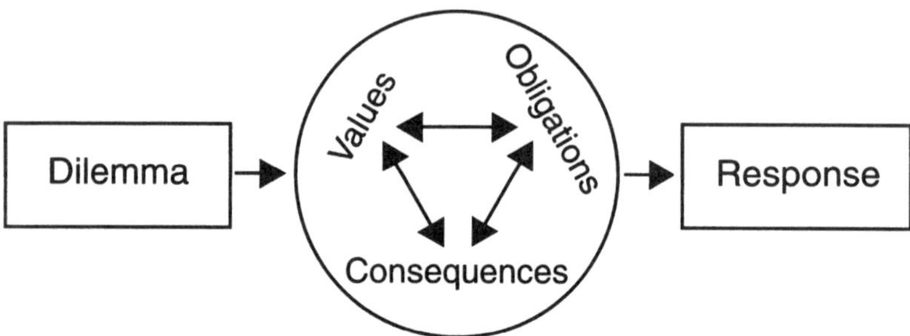

Figure 2.2 A model for ethical decision making (EDM)

The first two elements are similar to those in the original model (Brockett, 1988b) although they have been refined and expanded, while the third element has undergone considerable evolution from the initial operationalization of values dimension.

The most important difference from the earlier model, however, is that in the EDM model, ethical decision making is viewed as a cyclical rather than linear process. The above three elements are interactive and do not necessarily follow each other in a particular sequence. However, each needs to be considered.

An important aspect of ethical decision making is critical reflection. Usually when we make decisions, we are not even conscious of how we arrive at those decisions. Take the example of a jazz saxophone player who is improvising a solo. The musician is not consciously saying, "Now I'm going to play a Bb, then an E, now back to a D." Instead, the notes just seem to flow naturally. Similarly, it may seem a bit artificial to raise a series of questions that lead educators and trainers to consciously think through particular components of ethical decision making. In practice, we often act on a situation as it arises, using our best judgment. However, we believe that spelling out elements of the EDM model can help create awareness of the different components of ethical practice. In essence this means isolating key decision points that allow you to negotiate the decision making process and, ultimately, internalize the major questions underlying the process into your own repertoire of practice.

VALUES

- What do I believe?
  - About human nature?
  - About the education of adults?
  - About ethics?
- How committed am I to the beliefs I hold?
- Which basic values drive my practice?

OBLIGATIONS

- To whom am I responsible?
- To what extent does an ethical dilemma result from conflicting obligations?

CONSEQUENCES

- What are my options?
- What are the possible consequences of my actions?
- Which option is most consistent with my values?

Figure 2.3 Questions to guide ethical decision making

Before focusing on specific elements of the EDM model, it is important to reemphasize that this is a *process*, not a *prescriptive* technique. The model is not designed to provide specific answers for specific situations. Rather, it offers a basic guide for negotiating the process of resolving ethical dilemmas and help for educators and trainers of adults to begin thinking about how they might address ethical dilemmas in their own practice. With this caveat, here are the specific EDM model elements.

Values

A key element of ethical practice centers on the basic values that serve as a foundation for how we practice. According to Raths, Harmin, and Simon (1975, p. 72), values are "general guides to behavior" that "give direction to life." In describing the term *values*, Lewis (2000, p. 7) states "it should be synonymous with personal evaluations and personal beliefs, especially personal evaluations and related beliefs . . . that propel us to action, to a particular kind of behavior and life." Pojman (1995) suggests that a value can be described simply as "the quest for the good" (p. 82).

A concept that has received much attention in education literature particularly related to children, is values clarification. Simon (1993) describes the concept this way: "Values clarification is *a* process which helps people arrive at *an* answer. It is not concerned with an ultimate set of values . . . but it does stress a method to help you determine the content and power of *your* own set of values. It is . . . a tool to help you freely decide between alternatives or among varied choices" (p. xvi).

Values clarification, as described by Simon, Howe, and Kirschenbaum (1978), involves *choosing* freely from alternatives after considerable reflection, *prizing* and cherishing personal beliefs and affirming them publicly, and *acting* on personal beliefs in a consistent and repeated way. Values clarification has sometimes come under attack, particularly in elementary and secondary school settings, because it does not prescribe a single correct answer to a given dilemma. However, it is for this very reason that the approach is most consistent with what we advocate in the EDM model. We believe that values are best arrived at through critical reflection and careful consideration of alternative ways of looking at a situation. Here are three central questions to guide the process: What do I believe? How committed am I to the beliefs I hold? Which basic values drive my practice?

What Do I Believe?

An essential element of effective practice for educators and trainers of adults is a degree of self-understanding. Each of us has a belief system that drives how we practice—why we do what we do in a given situation. Often, however, we are not conscious of the rationale behind our actions. In graduate courses and workshops that both of us teach, we regularly challenge learners to identify and articulate core beliefs that drive their practice. By doing so, it is possible to understand the rationale behind many practices, identify points of incongruence between beliefs and actions, and expand the repertoire of practice by opening oneself to ideas or practices that had not been considered previously. With regard to ethical practice, we suggest that educators need to explore their beliefs relative to three main areas: (1) human nature, (2) the education of adults, and (3) ethics and moral obligation.

Among the most basic questions asked over the centuries by philosophers and more recently by psychologists are those that consider *beliefs about human nature*. Are people inherently "evil"? Are they inherently "good"? Is human nature essentially the product of one's environment? In the world of psychology, these three ways of viewing human nature roughly correspond to psychoanalytic theory, humanism, and behaviorism.

In terms of educational practice, the assumptions we make about human nature can drive how we work with learners. For instance, a teacher who takes a negative view of human nature may be more suspicious of the learners' motives. This can lead to using techniques designed to maximize instructor control of the classroom environment. On the other hand, a teacher who takes a positive outlook on human nature is likely to promote a learner-centered environment where trust and openness are stressed. Finally, a teacher who approaches practice from a behaviorist view will strive to shape a positive outcome by creating an environment that reinforces desirable characteristics while extinguishing undesirable ones.

Think about your own experiences as a learner. Can you recall teachers or trainers from each of these categories? We believe that each orientation has something to offer in working effectively with adult learners; however, our own values are most clearly grounded in the positive view of human nature reflected in humanistic thought (Hiemstra & Brockett, 1994). Regardless of how you eventually resolve the "human nature" question in your own mind, we believe it is crucial to your development as an effective, ethical educator or trainer to wrestle with your personal beliefs about human nature.

A second set of beliefs focuses on *the education of adults and the nature of adult learning*. What do I believe about the education of adults? What do I believe about adult learners? Such questions undergird a personal philosophy of adult education and training and can be linked, to a large degree, with the human nature assumptions mentioned above.

How do different belief systems play out in actual practice? Let's look at three hypothetical adult basic education (ABE) teachers who view what they do in very different ways. One teacher sees ABE as a remedial activity for individuals who have failed at previous efforts to learn basic skills. A second teacher views ABE as a strategy to address injustices resulting from oppression against certain groups, such as women, minorities, gays and lesbians, and people with disabilities. Still another teacher, involved in a corporate-sponsored workplace literacy program, views ABE as a means of increasing worker productivity and, hence, profitability. Clearly, each teacher approaches ABE from a different perspective. Similarly, each has the potential to be successful. However, it is likely that each teacher acts differently in working with learners and these differences are largely reflected in the basic values that drive their practice.

Thus, when thinking about personal values concerning the education of adults, you should ask these types of questions:

- Do I believe that adult learners are basically active or passive?
- Do I believe that adult learners have unlimited potential or that they engage in learning to overcome deficiencies or gaps in their knowledge, skills, or attitudes?
- Is my role as an instructor to serve as an expert or authority figure, a facilitator of the teaching and learning process, or a catalyst for social change?

Of course, such questions center on extreme positions and, as such, only scratch the surface, but they illustrate the wide range of perspectives of those engaged in educating and training adults.

Because the book's focus is primarily on ethical practice, an in-depth discussion of ethical theory is beyond the scope of this chapter. However, in order to understand our values as ethical decision-makers, we must distinguish between some fundamental differences in *beliefs about ethics and moral obligation.* Essentially, ethical theory has been driven by two major perspectives (Frankena, 1973; Pojman, 2001; Purtill, 1976; Thiroux, 1986).

One approach to ethics holds that rightness or wrongness depends on the consequences of personal actions. In other words, what is right produces good consequences. These theories are known as *teleological* (or consequential) theories. In teleological theories, ethical behavior is tied to self-interest: This can include self-interest of the person who is acting (ethical egoism), self-interest of someone other than the person who is acting (ethical altruism), or self-interest of everyone who is affected by the action (utilitarianism). In describing teleological theories, Kidder (1995) makes the following observation: "It demands of us a kind of cost-benefit analysis, determining who will be hurt and who helped and measuring the intensity of that help. It is the staple of public policy debate: Most legislation, these days, is crafted with this utilitarian test in mind" (p. 24).

A second approach to ethical theory holds that consequences should not be viewed as a criterion for determining what is right. Instead, *deontological* (or nonconsequential) theories are based on fulfilling personal duty, regardless of the consequences. Examples include fulfilling promises, performing specific roles or responsibilities, or divine command. Drawing from the principles of Immanuel Kant, this approach stresses the importance of following what you would want others to follow and, thus, creating a universal standard of behavior (Kidder, 1995). According to Kidder, deontological theories (sometimes called "rule-based thinking") can be understood as follows: "Never mind outcomes: Stick to your principles and let the consequential chips fall where they may. Based firmly on duty—on what we ought to do, rather than what we think might work—it is known among philosophers as *deontological* thinking, from the Greek word *deon*, meaning 'obligation' or 'duty' "(p. 24).

Here is a hypothetical example to clarify this distinction.

Bob is teaching a psychology class at a local community college. A large percentage of the final grade is based on attendance and active participation in the class. Ken, a part-time student who works full-time to support his family, has had to miss nearly one-third of the class sessions due to a highly stressful work situation involving additional evening hours at the time when the class meets. Were he not to work these hours, Ken believes he would risk losing his job. Ken's employer reimburses the tuition costs as long as he receives a grade of B or higher. Overall, Ken's written work in the course is a solid B. However, because Ken has missed so many class sessions, Bob is facing the dilemma of what to do.

Were he to act from a deontological framework, Bob would ask about the extent to which Ken lived by the rules of the agreement, regardless of mitigating circumstances. Bob might stress that Ken knew what his responsibilities were when he entered the course. Therefore, what is right is that Ken must fulfill the letter of the agreement regarding course expectations. In this case, assigning a lower final course grade is the "right" thing to do.

On the other hand, approaching the problem from a teleological framework, Bob would be inclined to consider the factors that mitigate this situation. For Ken, the consequences of attending class and not working might have included losing his job. Similarly, assigning a grade of lower than B would result in Ken not being reimbursed for the course by his employer. From a teleological, or consequentialist, perspective, Bob would likely look for a resolution that would produce the greatest good. This does not mean that he would simply assign Ken the higher grade. Indeed, this would probably violate institutional policies or expectations. However, Bob might consider giving Ken an incomplete and allow him an opportunity to do an alternative learning activity in lieu of the missed classes. By doing this, Bob allows Ken to complete the course and receive a grade that results in tuition reimbursement. The "greatest good" has been served by allowing Ken to fulfill his responsibilities while still upholding the academic standards of the course and institution.

So, to summarize, when engaging in ethical decision making it is important to have a clear sense of whether your decisions are driven more by what produces the best results for the greatest number of people or by your commitment to fulfill a specific duty or rule that you believe outweighs the consequences of your actions. It is crucial, therefore, to decide if you believe it is most important to base your ethical decisions on the possible consequences of your actions or on any rules and duties, irrespective of possible consequences.

How Committed Am I to the Beliefs I Hold?

A second question relative to the values dimension of the EDM model centers on the degree to which an educator or trainer is committed to particular values. Krathwohl, Bloom, and Masia (1964) point out that values can be incorporated into our lives, or "internalized," at three different levels. *Acceptance* of a value is tentative support for a particular belief. *Preference* for a value is much stronger; here the person actively pursues a position and is identified with it. *Commitment* to a value is a deeply held position often expressed as faith, loyalty, or conviction. Each of us internalizes our values at different levels; clarifying the level at which we internalize our values helps us understand those values we believe are truly worth standing up for.

To illustrate this let's look once again at adult basic education and consider whether receiving welfare benefits should be tied to mandatory participation. This issue has had major implications in recent years for ABE teachers, both in terms of whom such programs serve and how educators can work with students in the classroom setting.

As an example, think about three ABE teachers who oppose mandatory participation. Each has internalized their opposition at a different level and they are likely to express their opposition in very different ways.

At the lower end of commitment, Sue complains mildly about the frustration of diverting attention from more highly motivated learners to deal with participants who only want to put in time so that they can receive their benefits. Typically she keeps this complaint to herself and goes about her work, wishing that the policy could be changed. Paul, on the other hand, has internalized this issue at a deeper level. He voices his concerns openly in staff meetings, has presented his opposition at the annual conference of his state adult education association, and has contacted his state legislator to express his concerns. Jan's opposition is internalized at the level of "commitment." She believes the policy seriously compromises the quality of what she can do in the classroom; thus, she feels compelled to act on her commitment. Jan has considered several possible actions, including such extreme steps as quitting her job or even falsifying attendance records so that those participants who disrupt classes are "invited" to stay away without losing their welfare benefits.

The point here is that while all three teachers oppose the policy, each has different feelings about that opposition.

In considering the process of ethical decision making, we need to separate the proverbial wheat from the chaff. This can be accomplished by determining how deeply our values are internalized so we can choose our battles wisely and not spend excessive time or energy on concerns that are of less importance.

Which Basic Values Drive My Practice?

This is the third question relative to the values dimension of the EDM model. Clearly, there is no universal answer to this question, but the emphasis shifts toward those values most central to us as educators and trainers of adults. These are the values that serve as the bottom line for our practice. The educator who ignores this question risks inconsistencies between belief and action.

For the two of us, a number of values are central to how

we work with adult learners; two such values are respect and justice. First, we believe that *respect* is central to all we do as educators of adults. Respect is a nonjudgmental attitude that involves accepting and valuing a person as a unique individual. Rogers (1961) has referred to this notion as "unconditional positive regard." In practice, respect means an acceptance of others going beyond differences in backgrounds or values. Within our graduate classes and workshops, we often work with adults from extremely diverse backgrounds and orientations as they come from wide ranging practice settings such as community-based organizations, health and human services agencies, the military, public schools, churches, business and industry, agricultural extension, and proprietary schools. Thus, we recognize that our learners often have very different views about ideology and practice from our own. Yet by promoting the core value of respect, we can create an environment where divergent viewpoints thrive and actually stimulate critical reflection and the free exchange of ideas. Some of our most memorable and rewarding professional experiences have come through working with students whose ideological views differ dramatically from our own. Respect has made it possible for us to enjoy and grow from these experiences and, hopefully, also helped the learners develop and expand their awareness.

A second core value we share is commitment to *justice*. Justice, in the context of education and training for adults, involves actively promoting equity and access to educational opportunities. It is much more than mere tolerance of diversity based on race, gender, cultural background, or other differences. Instead, it involves actively embracing diversity to ensure that each learner has the best opportunity to gain as much as possible from any learning experience.

It essence, we believe it is crucial to reflect on personal values in order to uncover the core of who we are. In the next chapter, we present an approach to help you develop a personal philosophy relative to education and training with adults where you can identify and clarify those values central to your own practice. By doing so, you can personalize the key questions raised in the first dimension of the EDM model.

Obligations

A second dimension of the EDM model revolves around issues of responsibility and obligations. Two questions guide this dimension.

To Whom Am I Responsible?

In asking the question, "To whom am I responsible?" there are many possible answers. These include, but are not limited to the following:

- Ourselves
- The learners we serve
- The institutions that employ us
- Family and friends
- The profession
- Society

Sometimes, ethical conflicts develop because these roles and the corresponding responsibilities are not clearly defined. More often, however, problems develop when the roles are in conflict with each other. Stated another way, an ethical conflict arises whenever fulfilling an obligation to one party means not meeting an obligation to another party.

Conflicting responsibilities can lead to numerous ethical conflicts. The following are some examples:

- An extension agent must decide whether to advocate a specific position on the recertification of pesticide applicators or to facilitate a process that allows for alternate positions to be considered.
- A trainer is asked to befriend a group of fellow trainers who are against an unpopular policy that has recently been enacted by management.
- An evaluator is torn between wanting, on one hand, to present an honest assessment that can be used to improve a program serving a very real need in the community and, on the other hand, recognizing that a negative evaluation could lead to program elimination.

- A continuing education director whose program funding is driven by participant numbers may feel the need to develop certain programs that are likely to draw strong enrollments, but may be outside the basic mission of the institution.

To What Extent Does an Ethical Dilemma Result from Conflicting Obligations?

Purtilo and Cassel (1981) suggest that an ethical dilemma arises "when acting on one moral 'conviction' . . . means breaking another" (p.5). Often, ethical dilemmas develop when there are conflicting obligations due to the different roles that a person simultaneously holds (such as, classroom instructor and program administrator).

As was noted earlier in this chapter, Kidder (1995) argues that most ethical dilemmas are not a matter of right versus wrong, but rather, right versus right. He identifies four paradigms where this notion of right versus right is played out. These are as follows:

- Truth versus loyalty
- Individual versus community
- Short-term versus long-term
- Justice versus mercy

In adult education and training, these four paradigms are relevant whenever we ask ourselves where our greatest obligation lies. For instance, in the first paradigm a staff development coordinator asked by a supervisor to reveal the contents of an emotion-charged discussion during an in-service session may face a dilemma between telling the truth or responding in a way that honors loyalty to the discussion participants.

The second paradigm is one that is central to contemporary adult education practice (Beatty, 1992; Ilsley, 1992; Merriam & Brockett, 1997): Should the primary function of education or training be on individual-based personal growth or community-based social change? One illustration of this paradigm, as applied to decisions concerning the funding of adult education, is "the distinction between striving for the goal of 'education for all' and directing limited financial and human resources toward those who, it is generally believed, will make the most of such opportunities" (Merriam & Brockett, 1997, p. 288).

The third paradigm, short-term versus long-term, has clear relevance to education and training for adults in terms of such issues as setting goals, determining funding priorities, and creating a vision for the future. For example, how does an ABE teacher resolve potential conflict between helping learners meet a short-term goal of passing the General Education Development (GED) examination and the longer-term goal of helping the learner develop skills that lead to self-sufficiency? This example is discussed more fully in the next section. Or, how does a dean of continuing education in a state university balance the immediate need to show increased enrollments with a desire to create dynamic new programs that, over the course of several years, have the potential to grow and add to enrollments and the institution's reputation?

Finally, the justice-versus-mercy paradigm comes into play whenever a person must decide how to respond to wrongdoing (potential or actual) or situations in which there are extenuating circumstances. An example of this is where a teacher must decide what to do about a student who has failed to complete course assignments because of being preoccupied with facing the final stages of a loved one's terminal illness. Should the instructor follow the letter of the law, under the guise of justice, or demonstrate mercy by making allowances due to circumstances beyond the student's control?

Each of these four paradigms shows that in so many ethical dilemmas there may not be a single appropriate course of action. Instead, we often must choose among alternatives. Along with this comes the recognition that each choice we make is likely to have a different set of potential consequences. This brings us to the remaining dimension of the EDM model.

Consequences

An educator or trainer who faces an ethical dilemma almost always has more than one choice. Simply stated, if there were no choice, there would be no dilemma. Of course, some choices are more desirable than others. Being able to assess possible consequences of different choices and to make decisions about which choices are most desirable is central to ethical decision making. Three questions can help you focus:

1. What are my options?

2. What are the possible consequences of my actions?

3. Which option is most consistent with my values?

When examining this dimension of the EDM model, it is first necessary to identify all possible options. If it is possible to do so, begin with a brainstorming process where each possibility is listed or identified. At this point, it is not necessary to evaluate the options, but rather, simply to list them.

To illustrate this dimension, let us consider the case of Samantha, a GED instructor who has been told that the focus of her job will shift from helping learners obtain the GED to teaching basic skills that will help them gain employment. Samantha is very disturbed by this changing policy because she believes that the GED can help her students gain greater long-term self-sufficiency than will skills for a minimum wage job with little chance of advancement. However, her supervisor is faced with pressure to show that participants are moving quickly through the program and finding successful employment; therefore, Samantha has been told to immediately shift the focus of her classes.

Samantha has several choices or courses of action. These could include the following:

1. Accept the decision and comply with the policy.

2. Reflect on the situation and change her position on the issue.

3. Try to change the policy through established channels by providing data or other evidence to support her position.

4. Continue to focus on GED instruction and "cover up" what she is actually doing.

5. Leave the organization.

The key here, as with any ethical decision, is to recognize that every choice comes with consequences. And most options come with more than one possible set of consequences. Thus, once the full range of options has been identified, it is time to go back and evaluate the potential of each option by reflecting on the question, "What are the possible consequences of my actions?"

Of course, for the dilemma that Samantha must address, some options are more viable than others. For example, one consequence of the first option is that Samantha's job will remain safe and she can continue her work with the mandated changes. Another consequence, though, is that Samantha may feel that she is selling out and compromising her commitment to the learners she is serving. With the second option, there is likely to be little conflict since Samantha has been convinced that the policy is a good one; of course, if her opposition to the policy is strong to begin with, this option may not be viable from the outset. In the third option, one consequence may be that Samantha is able to provide evidence to convince her supervisor that the policy is not in the best interest of the learners; at the same time, another consequence of this option could be frustration and futility at spending time and energy on something that might not even have a chance to be heard. The fourth option can be particularly tricky, since it involves some degree of deception on Samantha's part. Here, Samantha has the possibility of continuing to serve the learners in the way she believes is to their greatest benefit; however, she does so knowing that there could be serious negative consequences if the supervisor learns of her actions. Finally, the fifth option provides the possibility of both positive and negative consequences. On the positive side, Samantha is able to publicly stand by her principles and, thus, know that she has acted with a high level of integrity. At the same time, leaving the organization will deprive the students of their teacher and leave Samantha with no job, which can lead to other consequences for her and other family members who depend on her income.

What should Samantha do? It is beyond the scope of the EDM model to prescribe a specific course of action for a specific person in a specific situation. Hopefully, however, by using the

EDM model, Samantha can carefully consider the full range of her obligations—to her students, her employer, her family (who will be directly affected should she lose her job), and herself—and the basic values that drive her practice. By reflecting on the full range of possibilities and eventually zeroing in on what is most important to her, Samantha is hopefully able to arrive at a decision that, while probably not ideal, is nonetheless one she is able and willing to own and from which she is able to accept whatever consequences may result. In Chapter 5, we discuss a process and provide a worksheet that can assist you in working through options and possible consequences in your own dilemmas.

CONCLUSION

Ethical decision making is not easy. As we continue to show throughout the book, it often takes great courage to make ethical decisions—to "do the right thing." We believe there is no simple formula for the right answer to specific ethical dilemmas. However, in presenting the EDM model, we hope we have helped you understand ethical decision making as a process of reflection and action centering on three key focal points. For each of these, several questions can help to guide your thinking about what is most important. Ultimately, it is this question of importance that leads us to make decisions that we can stand by with a sense of integrity and commitment, regardless of the ultimate consequences. In the next chapter, we show how ethical decision making permeates the education and training of adults.

CHAPTER 3

Ethical Issues in Practice

In Chapter 2 we presented a model for ethical decision making (EDM) designed to help educators and trainers of adults raise questions appropriate for negotiating their way through situations where potential exists for ethical conflict. We recognize there are times when instant decisions are required and the notion of employing a process becomes almost moot. Kidder (1995), for instance, describes a situation where a state police officer comes upon an accident in which a truck driver is hopelessly pinned inside a burning cab. The driver pleads with the officer to shoot him because he is in agonizing pain. Facing the personal conflict this situation created with his own moral principles and ethical beliefs, the officer finally finds a way of relieving the man's suffering by rendering him unconscious with fire extinguisher fumes but without taking his life with a bullet. Even though the man dies from the ensuing fire, the officer was able to humanely deal with the situation without violating his own ethical beliefs.

Obviously, the chance of any one of us as a professional educator facing such a life or death struggle is remote. But we do face instances where immediate decisions are required even in the face of potential ethical conflicts. For example, a trainer suddenly recognizes a front-end need analysis was way off track and participants in an expensive training session quickly require something different if the experience is to be successful. A teacher in an ABE classroom recognizes that one student is becoming very uncomfortable with personal questions raised by fellow students during a get-acquainted activity. As we face such conflicts between our values in relation to appropriate educational content and our obligations to others as learners or even as individuals outside the educational arena, some rapid decisions may need to be made.

Roger experienced such a situation during an intensive weeklong summer workshop for which he was the instructor.

It became clear during the very first couple of hours that one of the participants, a new student, was having emotional difficulties dealing with group discussion and subsequent learning activities. Her behavior deteriorated throughout that first morning as she began interrupting others as they tried to talk, left her chair and walked around the room to peer at the handwritten notes of fellow students, and raised questions that did not appear to relate to the class topic. At one point she sat down in the middle of the room (chairs had been arranged in a circle) and demanded that everyone join her there in discussing the merits of the class. It was clear everyone was becoming very uncomfortable with the situation even though the instructor attempted to work with the behavior.

Going through the instructor's mind were the obligations due all members of the class for a good learning experience in juxtaposition with what he valued in terms of respect for each person and each person's individuality. Knowing a decision needed to be made, at a midmorning break he moved quietly among the other students and told them he would dismiss the class quite early for an extended lunch period so the situation could be dealt with. He also asked for their complete confidentiality in terms of not discussing the experience with others. He quickly asked an experienced student in the class to go to lunch with the troubled student if she wanted company. The troubled student opted to go home for lunch, since she lived near campus.

Soon after the break period he announced that students would have a couple hours in which they could visit the library, work with each other in formulating learning plans, eat their lunch, and so forth. As soon as the students left the classroom he went to the university's Counseling Center and asked for an immediate audience with any available counselor. They quickly discussed the circumstances and the counselor agreed to attempt to reach a family member of the troubled student. Fortunately, a family member was reached by phone and when the situation was explained, it was agreed the family would seek professional help for the loved one. It was later learned the student was hospitalized that day for a nervous breakdown.

Upon returning to the classroom after lunch, the instructor and students spent considerable time discussing the morning's experience, how it was dealt with, and the various ethical ramifications. It was a workshop on self-directed learning so some valuable discussion centering on individual rights, facilitator roles, and dealing with unusual teaching and learning experiences was both appropriate and meaningful. All students pledged to keep confidential the specific circumstances of the morning. In the final workshop evaluations, several students commented on how much they had learned about ethical behavior and facilitator skills from the experience.

These types of experiences raise the important question, "To whom am I responsible as an educator of adults?" We like to think that the word "responsible" can also be pronounced "response-able." In essence, this means, are we able to have a response that is appropriate for a situation or dilemma, is ethically sound, and even is fairly rapid if the situation warrants it?

We hope that the EDM model described in this book becomes one you will practice until it becomes incorporated into your professional repertoire and helps prevent "seat-of-the-pants" or spur of the moment decision making that does not include ethical considerations. We believe that with practice you can incorporate ethical decision making into your normal teaching or training approach and the type of quick response suggested above becomes second nature.

Thus, this chapter contains insight on ethical issues dealing with our practice as professional educators or trainers of adults. We begin by providing a framework for understanding why we deal with practice issues the way we do. It is based on our contention that personal philosophical beliefs serve as a foundation for how we address any ethical issues. Two sections that describe specific areas of practice in which the EDM model can be employed follow this. In the first section we offer a discussion of several aspects of teaching or training where potential ethical issues or dilemmas are possible. We conclude by describing various program planning and implementation components as well as potential ethical issues.

DEVELOPING A STATEMENT
OF PERSONAL PHILOSOPHY

As we already noted in the first two chapters, personal values, beliefs, and corresponding value systems serve as basic steppingstones to subsequent ethical practice and behavior. Essentially, they become a foundation for how we practice. We believe that even if they are not recognized consciously, these steppingstones affect how and why we make the ethical decisions we do: "This recognition of personal values, beliefs, and the various changes a person undergoes throughout life, if combined with a personal philosophy statement, can result in foundational tools useful as guides or mirrors for subsequent professional actions and ethical decision-making" (Hiemstra, 1988, p. 178).

Hiemstra (1988) goes into considerable detail on how to create a statement of personal philosophy. Also Hiemstra (2002b) provides a website that details additional material as well as some sample statements of philosophy. Appendix A at the end of this chapter outlines a workshop for teaching others how to create personal philosophy statements. Regarding one's philosophy, Boulmetis (1999) asks the question: How can you know you're doing it if you don't know what it is? Tisdell and Taylor (1999) also describe how various adult education philosophies inform practice.

Thus, if you have not already created a personal philosophy statement, or if it has been several years since you have done so, we recommend that you utilize something like the process shown in Appendix A or in the Hiemstra (1988) chapter as part of your efforts to enhance personal ethical decision-making abilities. We believe you will find this both revealing and helpful in matching your practice with your beliefs and your ethics.

ETHICAL DILEMMAS IN TEACHING AND TRAINING ADULTS

In Chapter 2 we said it is important to determine which values are so central they drive our practice. Kidder (1994) describes several core values important to a universal understanding of ethics: love, truth, fairness, freedom, unity, tolerance, responsibility, and respect of life. Several, if not all, of these values relate directly to the teaching or training of adults.

In fact, it has been our observation and experience that a person's values impact on professional practice in many different ways. For example, a teacher grounded in humanistic beliefs (Brockett, 1997; Hiemstra & Brockett, 1994) will place emphasis on a learner's ability to use previous experiences in order to understand their learning needs (Hiemstra, 1997; Hiemstra & Sisco, 1990; Sisco, 1997) and involve them in determining the instructional content. On the other hand, a trainer who relies primarily on behaviorism (Skinner, 1954; Tyler, 1974) might predetermine most of a workshop's content and expect all participants to follow the same educational content as they progress through the learning experience.

Thus, the questions of what do I believe and how committed am I to these beliefs, can present ethical dilemmas in various ways, depending on organizational expectations, learner needs, and any instructional requirements. The potential for ethical conflict exists throughout the entire teaching and learning experience. What are some of those ethical issues or dilemmas facing the teachers of adults?

McDonald and Wood (1993) conducted a survey of various adult education populations and found that the three most frequently cited ethical dilemma areas were confidentiality, ownership of instructional material, and employment practices. Clement, Pinto, and Walker (1978) reported on an earlier study where lack of professional development, violation of confidences, and the use of "cure-all" programs were the top three areas identified by a group of trainers. Figures 3.1 and 3.2 provide additional questions for you to ponder. We recommend that you create your own list of questions or potential ethical dilemmas and utilize the EDM model to work through ways of dealing with any concomitant issues.

This chapter presents three questions to illustrate how ethical conflicts can arise. The first question relates to the role of the teacher as expert versus that as a facilitator. The second question deals with the nature of personal versus professional relationships between teachers and students. The last question pertains to the nature of how material is presented.

Should teachers or trainers agree to present subject matter with which they are largely unfamiliar, even when pressured to do so because of a perceived or mandated need?

Wilson (1982) elaborates on this dilemma by adding the question, if the answer is yes, should the teacher or trainer pretend to know the content better than they do so learners feel they are getting everything they should from an expert? Scriven (1982) also wonders whether teachers should present material that they have not updated for some time. Most of us have probably been in a situation where the presenter was neither knowledgeable nor up to date, but refused to admit it.

Thus, at the heart of how we teach or train adults is the notion of what kind of a role the teacher or trainer should play. As Caffarella (1988) notes, some people advocate facilitating a learning process where considerable self-direction on the part of the learner is possible, while others argue for a role of teacher as content expert (Grasha, 1994; Reinsmith, 1994). Obviously, whether you agree mainly with one belief system or the other, or fall somewhere in between, you are likely to encounter ethical issues or dilemmas as you work with learners.

Consider the instance in a higher education setting where faculty cutbacks or a freeze on hiring requires very few faculty in a small department to teach all courses in the curriculum so

Ethical Questions Related to Teaching and Training Adults

How do you ensure that materials used or distributed in a classroom are referenced appropriately?

How do you deal with situations where learners are required to participate against their wishes?

How do you deal with learners who have been found or are suspected to be cheating?

How do you deal with learners who take advantage of or abuse an educational system or process?

How do you deal with learners who do not live up to their potential?

How much should a teacher or trainer be available to learners outside formal meeting times?

How do you deal with obvious cultural, gender, or special needs while still being fair to other learners?

Should learners be required to complete certain forms, instruments, or inventories that are deemed essential to the learning process?

Should learners be given multiple options or alternatives as opposed to specific learning requirements?

To what extent should teachers or trainers share their personal views and beliefs on an issue?

How should issues of privacy and confidentiality be handled in dealing with learners?

Figure 3.1 Questions with potential for ethical conflict in teaching adults

**Ethical Questions Related to Planning and
Implementing Programs for Adults**

How can educators negotiate the politics of the planning process when there is conflict between an agency's mission or procedures and learners' desires?

How do you deal with conflicts of interest between needed program content and the wishes or preferences of funding sources?

How do you deal with mandated curricular objectives in light of learner needs and expectations that are different?

Are there times when compulsory participation by adult learners is justifiable?

What do you do when you know evaluation results have been fabricated or altered?

Should evaluators always declare their identities to subjects or is covert evaluation ever justified?

Should evaluators report all harmful practices or effects they observe?

What types of success claims or expectations should be advertised as expected educational program results?

What type of confidentiality should be maintained on information known about adult learners?

Should an educational program always be based on a front-end needs analysis or are there instances when program decisions can be made on institutional traditions?

What are the best ways of evaluating teachers or trainers and how do you use the resulting information?

What criteria should an administrator use in hiring teachers or trainers? Should there be different criteria for hiring part-time versus full-time people?

Figure 3.2 Questions with potential for ethical conflict in planning programs

students do not have difficulties finishing their program within an expected time period. You, in such a situation, might be required to teach a course you have never taught before. This may mean you recognize the learning experience for students will be less than it could be with a more knowledgeable professor. In some subject matter areas where highly technical content or specialized materials are involved, this could be even more problematic. The ethical dilemma for you is how do you let students know about the possible limitations, especially when important core values you hold are honesty and telling the truth to others.

Using the EDM model, you might ask yourself, "To whom am I most responsible?" If the answer is the learners, then one consequence might be the decision to let students know at the beginning of the course about your own limitations and then give them the option to delay taking the course until a later date. Then, you can work with those who remain in designing a process where you all learn as much as you can together about the subject matter and even find a way of using outside experts. On the other hand, if you feel most responsible to the institution, you may need to gloss over certain material this first time and require that students carry out extra reading in those areas you admit to having knowledge limitations.

Another situation could involve you as a trainer who one morning is handed the printout of a PowerPoint® presentation, including a script with accompanying small-group tasks. You are asked by the director of training to conduct the afternoon workshop on a topic you have never before delivered. Your ethical dilemma centers on the following: (1) you are against canned presentations to begin with because they do not take into account the individuality of each learner, and (2) you firmly believe in being involved with a front-end analysis prior to designing an instructional unit. Based on the director's few comments you suspect no advanced assessment of need was carried out. The conflicting responsibilities you feel toward both the participants and your supervisor result in considerable personal angst. Critically reflecting on the situation with the EDM model, you decide on an option that is most consistent with what you value as a trainer.

You begin the session with an informal assessment of what participants need most from the afternoon. After summarizing the most critical needs identified by participants, you are able to use a portion of the PowerPoint® presentation, but you change the small-group activities so that participants can further discuss what they need. You also help them determine their own future learning activities and conclude the session by determining what additional information you can provide them through e-mail messages and appropriate attachments over the next few days.

In both of these examples, the educator used a process to think through values, obligations, and consequences that resulted in more open communication with participants, a non-confrontational approach, and a path through the teaching and learning experience that was responsive rather than prescriptive. More important each educator recognized that ethical dilemmas, unless dealt with, could have created feelings of being less than "response-able."

What should be the proper professional distance between teachers or trainers and the learners with whom they work?

Most of us want to be liked by others and the tendency to be personable to enhance that desire is natural. We are not suggesting that a teacher or trainer remain completely aloof from participants in a class or workshop, but care must be taken in developing relationships outside the educational setting. The two of us started out in a teacher-student relationship, but mutual respect and admiration over time lead to a mentor-mentee relationship and ultimately a close friendship and collegial and coauthoring associations. We describe our personal experience in greater detail elsewhere (Hiemstra & Brockett, 1998).

As instructors we both establish an informal atmosphere in the classroom where first names are encouraged to initiate a process of mutual respect, but we take care that the teacher- student relationship is maintained. A power differential always remains between teacher and student because of perceptions about status, level of expertise, and ultimate institutional expectations about evaluation of learning. Letting a mutual respect turn to a close friendship too quickly is ripe for various ethical dilemmas.

Willing, Morford, and Haney (1998) provide ten useful tips for maintaining appropriate professional boundaries with adult students:

1. Know your own personal vulnerabilities, personality type, motivation, and expectation of others.

2. Understand that the teacher-student relationship is almost always temporary.

3. Know professional and institutional standards for behaviors toward students.

4. Understand differences in the expectations of roles across cultures.

5. Recognize the messages you convey to students by touch, language, and self-disclosure.

6. Make clear your time boundaries by establishing how and when you will meet with learners outside a formal class period or setting.

7. Recognize how various students may interpret differently real or perceived relationships.

8. Assess your expectations regarding the use of first names, nicknames, and titles and how they may be perceived by learners.

9. Understand that how a teacher dresses or appears conveys various messages to learners.

10. Know the resources available for referral and how to help learners access them when needed.

For example, professional boundaries are potentially more crucial and often more complex between people of different gender.

> *Ginny, a skilled trainer for a major manufacturing company, was especially talented in stand-up delivery techniques. After one session when others had left, a remaining workshop participant asked if they could go get a cup of*

coffee so he could ask her about her delivery style and how she had developed it. Over her years as a trainer, Ginny had developed her own three foot rule in that she attempted to move no closer than three-feet from a participant unless some particular technique required it. She believed that ethically she owed this to others so no one would ever believe she crossed the line between her personal and professional roles. She resolved this potential dilemma by asking him for his e-mail user id and agreeing to send him some material she had developed on stand-up delivery approaches and to dialogue electronically if he had questions.

Another area for possible misunderstanding centers on cultural differences between teacher and learner.

Glenn was a professor of adult education and he frequently used simulation techniques in the classroom. Early in a graduate course on adult learning he divided the class members into pairs. He asked each person to practice interviewing the partner with an interview guide he wanted them to use later in interviewing people outside of class. The purpose was to gather information on the types of learning activities adults had been involved with over the course of a year.

One pair consisted of a person from Indonesia and one from the United States. Glenn noticed immediately that the Indonesian student seemed distressed and very uncomfortable in answering questions posed by the other student. Ethically Glenn was committed to having both students obtain a good learning experience out of the practice opportunity, but he valued the right of any student to opt out of a particular activity. Glenn intervened by asking the Indonesian student if he could take his place as interviewee to help the other student practice the questioning technique. He also asked the Indonesian student if he would observe the simulated interviews and then they could work out an alternative learning experience, which they did at the conclusion of that class session. Because of discomfort with English and unfamiliarity with simulation techniques, the student explained his confusion and uneasiness. Glenn then

> *helped him devise a strategy for talking with other Indonesian students on campus about informal learning they had done before starting graduate school.*

What should teachers or trainers do to stay current with constantly changing information?

Most teachers or trainers of adults put in long hours of class preparation, working with learners, attending meetings, and dealing with various other responsibilities. Finding time to read the most recent issue of a professional journal, do research on the Web to find the current thinking on a topic, or attend a conference can be difficult. As mentioned earlier, Clement, Pinto, and Walker (1978) reported that the most frequently mentioned unethical behavior observed by training and development professionals was a lack of professional development.

Yet, ethically, what do we owe our learners and ourselves in terms of current information on the knowledge base for which we are responsible? The following scenario illustrates this question:

> *Harold taught the same introductory course to graduate students almost every term for many years. He was very busy with many advising, research, and university committee responsibilities. There never seemed to be enough time in the day to get everything done. It would be so easy to use the same lecture notes from term to term. However, he was committed to a personal value of staying up-to-date on each subject he taught. Thus, he spent many evenings and weekends reading his professional journals, sought out new books on his topics, tried to present related papers at a professional conference each year, and engaged in a steady regimen of publishing that facilitated his keeping current. He believes both he and his students benefit from his various efforts.*

The complexities of the teaching and learning process are not made easier by knowing that ethical decisions may be required from time to time. However, as has been demonstrated by the vignettes described above, having a framework for decision making that you can use when wrestling with a potential dilemma can provide a peace of mind that helps counter some of the complexity.

ETHICAL ISSUES IN PLANNING AND IMPLEMENTING PROGRAMS

Planning and implementing programs for adult learners can seem fairly straightforward in many respects. Often, learner needs will drive instructional and learning objectives. These, in turn, result in educational programs. Skilled planners also carry out various forms of evaluation and administrators oversee the implementation of these various efforts. Yet, the planning and implementing of programs do not take place in isolation. This is usually an interactive process involving several players, or stakeholders, and driven by values of learners, teachers or trainers, administrators, the sponsoring organization, and even society. Sork (1988) describes it this way:

> Program planning is a complex decision-making process that results in the production of outcome and design specifications for systematic learning experiences. Many of the necessary decisions involve making choices among mutually exclusive ends and means, each of which is associated with a value position. Ethical issues arise in program planning when any of the alternatives under consideration are associated with value positions that may be viewed as unacceptable by society, other practitioners, clients, sponsors, or planners themselves. (p. 34)

The competing views of what is or is not acceptable, based on differing values, can turn a straightforward process into a potential ethical quagmire and, as Cervero and Wilson (1994) point out, this takes place in a context where issues of power exist. When this happens the importance of negotiation is crucial.

In this section we again present several questions designed to illustrate ways the EDM model can help us through the quagmire. The first question revolves around involving learners in the planning process. The second one relates to the type of needs that should serve to stimulate subsequent program or instructional efforts. The third question deals with some of the complexities in evaluating programs. A final question pertains to issues of profit and how monies are used. Refer to Figures 3.1 and 3.2 for additional questions to stimulate your thinking about possible issues you may face.

Is it always necessary to involve learners in the planning process?

Deciding who will be involved in any planning effort can be a difficult task. Knowles (1980, 1986), for example, long advocated that learners should be involved in planning their own learning, designing their own learning contracts, and even validating their own learning outcomes. Others can be involved, too, such as administrators, program sponsors, and outside experts. Sork (1988) suggests that various ethical issues can arise when deciding who will be involved and on the nature of this involvement. Wilson and Cervero (1996) suggest we must take care regarding who even sits at the planning table: "Our ethical stance is that all people who are affected by the program should be involved in the real choices of constructing the program, not just called up as information sources or used to justify already-made decisions" (p. 22).

> *Bruce, a county extension agent working in northern Iowa, faced exactly such an issue. He had made it a habit to solicit potential participant feedback throughout the planning process via a number of committees he had established. Thus, when the Federal Extension Service sent out a "canned" program on new types of corn borers, an emerging problem in several southern states, he immediately took it to his agronomy advisory committee. Members of the committee recognized it could be a future problem, but what they advised as most needed was information on how to grow organic corn, as there was a growing market for that product in the bigger cities.*
>
> *When Bruce approached his regional supervisor he was told they must deliver the federally mandated programs in all counties or face the possibility of reduced funding. Ethically he was committed to accepting advice from potential*

participants in designing programs, but he also felt a real allegiance to the Iowa Extension Service. Understanding the potential consequences of not delivering the mandated program, he worked with the agronomy advisory committee and they planned a half-day Saturday workshop for interested farmers, rather than a typical two-hour evening session. The advertising material for the workshop made it clear they would cover the potential for new types of corn borers in Iowa because of a growing problem in several other states. However, it was also made clear that recommendations of the advisory committee would be followed and information also provided on how to convert some of the current corn acreage into organic corn for the emerging markets. A better than normal turnout and positive evaluations indicated that correct decisions had been made.

This issue can emerge at the classroom level, too.

Cheryl, a GED preparation teacher for a local welfare-to-work program, was having difficulty with the progress students were making in her classroom. Even though attendance was mandated by the governmental agency that had established the program, participants seemed to be periodically absent, frequently late, or, when there, often uninterested in the subject matter. Cheryl was a committed teacher and felt ethically responsible for the students and their success. She thought about these obligations and her own values and philosophy as a teacher and decided to try a radical change. She began working with students to help them design a learning program that was self-paced and built around specific interests they had. Although she had to make some adjustments in her normal teaching style, the students gained a new motivation and actually began moving through the material quicker than they ever had before.

These examples show the complexity of what on the surface appears to be a given in working with adult learners. While most educators of adults would agree that learners should be involved in the planning process, there are instances when this will not always be the case.

To what extent should educators respond to the perceived needs of learners?

Besides determining who should be involved in assessing needs, another question that most program planners must face is how to address the struggle between what learners perceive are their educational needs versus what can be determined to be real or actual needs. Sork (1988) raises several questions we should consider pertaining to both types of needs. Sisco (1988) refers to this as an ethical dilemma in terms of meeting the client's needs versus the institution's needs.

Long (Hiemstra & Long, 1974) carried out a research study on physical therapists in Nebraska so he could design an appropriate continuing education program for them. He began by addressing their perception of need through a questionnaire in which subjects were asked what they felt they needed to learn. Their potential needs were also determined via answers they gave on how to best solve problems detailed in case studies on injuries young people had obtained while playing high school sports. In addition, Long also asked a panel of experts to suggest the most appropriate continuing education needs for a group of physical therapists.

He found significant discrepancies among all three data-gathering approaches, but finally concluded that ethically he was bound to design continuing education programs based on all three sources of information. Consequently, the perceived needs were used as initial training topics. He also added other topics as more advanced materials based both on some errors found in answers supplied for the case studies and on those suggestions made by experts in the field. As often is the case in situations where competing needs are at issue, is it ethical for educators to try and understand whose voices are being heard and whose are not?

Are there instances when it is justifiable to withhold information obtained through program evaluation efforts?

This question at times can indicate a real dilemma exists, especially if badly needed funding might be lost should a program not live up to its initial billing. House (1996a) notes that ethical issues surface when you must decide who will be the beneficiary of the evaluation information. It may be tempting to simply hand the information to a manager and leave it at that, especially if that manager awards future research and evaluation contracts. However, it is also important to take into consideration the interests of clients, program recipients, and even society at large when disseminating evaluation information.

Aaron faced exactly this problem when he agreed to serve as an outside evaluator midway through a four-year international project in an African country aimed at teaching villagers how to develop new cottage industries within their region. He was one of three people from the United States who were teamed with three people from within the country and charged with the evaluation effort. After spending three weeks gathering information from villagers who had participated in the training program, the project's in-country trainers, government officials responsible for the project, and the development specialists themselves, the team was given a week to prepare an evaluation report.

It was quickly made clear by both the development specialists and the government officials that continuation funding could be affected by outcomes of the evaluation effort. Aaron also observed that two of the in-country members of the team and some of the development specialists were making efforts to keep out of the report some less than flattering information about the trainers' skills. They suggested all such problems could be corrected with continued funding. Although Aaron struggled some with what his stance should be, he believed the obligations he owed ultimately to the villagers to ensure for them the best possible training program took top priority. Thus, he argued forcefully and strongly for full disclosure throughout the report, much to the consternation of some team members. The project did receive continuation funding, but recommendations in the report that the trainers receive additional training on how to teach adults meant money had to be redirected and not all original objectives could be achieved. Another consequence was that Aaron was not asked again by the international development agency to serve as an evaluator. Perhaps most important from an ethical sense is that Aaron concluded his work with the project feeling he had made the right decisions.

Should all continuing education efforts be profitable?

At face value the answer to such a question seems axiomatic. Of course an organization cannot operate for long if it is running at a deficit and prudent managers may not see any ethical issues involved with decisions about profit and loss. However, if only short-term goals aimed at ensuring profit are pursued, what long-term interests of clients or even society may be missed (Price, 1997)? This is a good example of what Kidder (1995) identified as long-term versus short-term dilemmas, which was discussed in Chapter 2.

Cervero and Wilson (1994) suggest that an effective administrator must be ethically responsible to everyone who may be affected by an adult education program. Huber (1997) says that an ethical approach for managers is "making sure others' needs are served so that they grow as persons, while not further depriving the least privileged in society." (p. 30)

One of us experienced this issue directly (Hiemstra, 1971).

Roger was hired to serve as director of an evening noncredit continuing education program. His supervisor made it clear at his hiring that the overall program efforts must be self-sustaining, including covering all administrative and instructional costs. In the past this had meant offering courses aimed primarily at attracting large numbers and subjecting all courses to a rule that if a certain number of registrations were not reached by a certain date, the course would be dropped.

Hired in the spring to put together a fall and winter term program, he began by carrying out a needs assessment through a survey he mailed to all attendees of past courses.

The fall term contained courses that seemed to best meet the majority of needs uncovered during the needs survey. However, as the course cancellation date approached, two of the courses had insufficient numbers. Fortunately, one of the courses had attracted a very large number of students. Because he felt obligated to meet all learners' needs, Roger successfully lobbied his supervisor to continue the lower en-rolled courses based on the profits that would be garnered from the one course. As a consequence this actually resulted in an institutional policy change that permitted profits from successful courses to be used in funding other courses.

Program planning and implementation efforts can be contentious at times. There will be disagreements on approaches to use, the specific directions programs should take, funding issues, and even how to interpret program outcomes. However, it can be very reassuring to have a model for ethical decision making available to work through some of the resulting stress and to be a means for justifying some of the decisions you do make.

CONCLUSION

In this chapter we stressed the importance of understanding your own philosophical views and stance as an educator or trainer of adults. Such an understanding enhances your ability to make consistent ethical decisions. We also utilized two areas of practice, teaching or training adults and planning programs for adults, to demonstrate that various ethical dilemmas are possible. We suggested how the EDM model can be helpful in working through various dilemmas to arrive at ethically sound decisions. In the next chapter we continue this approach by using the model to describe how such decisions can be made in five common concerns or areas that may impact each of us at different times in our career.

CHAPTER 4

Common Concerns:
Five Ethical Dilemmas

In the previous chapter, we identified ethical dilemmas that can arise in different areas of adult education and training practice. However, there are many ethical concerns that transcend a particular aspect of practice as well as a particular practice setting. We refer to these as common concerns because they have implications for everyone engaged in the education or training of adults. In this chapter, we describe five issues we believe exemplify such common concerns: (1) advocacy for social change, (2) technology, (3) censorship, (4) marketing, and (5) self-directed learning. For each area, we begin by exploring some of the background and contexts relative to potential dilemmas. This is followed by a set of questions that could be asked about each dilemma using the model for ethical decision making (EDM).

While we could have selected any number of relevant areas as common concerns, we believe that these five issues include a combination of classic areas of potential conflict as well as more contemporary areas of concern. Furthermore, one of the areas, censorship, is included because while little has been written about this topic in the context of adult education and training, we view it as a real threat to ethical practice that is often overlooked or ignored. Thus, as you read this chapter, we encourage you to think about other broad-ranging issues that you face in your work or life and to analyze corresponding dilemmas in a similar way.

ADVOCACY FOR SOCIAL CHANGE

From its earliest days as a professional field, adult education has struggled with questions regarding the extent to which educators or trainers of adults should be involved in promoting social change. Lindeman (1989/1926), in his seminal work *The Meaning of Adult Education*, made a clear statement on behalf of social change from a Deweyan progressive perspective. Stewart (1987), in a biography suggested one of Lindeman's "basic beliefs was that adult education was the most reliable instrument for social activists" (p. 51). Other early examples of education for social change included Jane Addams's work in the Chicago area with Hull-House (Addams, 1930), the Bryn Mawr Summer School for Women Workers (Heller, 1984), and other efforts to train women workers in the 1930s and 40s (Kornbluh & Frederickson, 1984).

Perhaps the best-known example of education for social change within the United States is reflected in the work of the Highlander Research and Education Center (originally the Highlander Folk School) in Tennessee, which was established in 1932 to provide education on organizing unions (Adams, 1975; Horton, Kohl, & Kohl, 1990). Eventually, Highlander played a vital role in the civil rights movement of the 1950s and 1960s and later as a resource for educators concerned with environmental and economic issues from a community-based perspective. In the late nineties it even served as the venue for female professors of adult education to meet and discuss common concerns (Hansman & Mott, 1999).

Cotton (1964) described a historic divide that has existed between "social reform" and "professional" traditions of adult education. The former tradition views adult education as a vehicle for addressing the "great social, political and economic issues confronting their respective societies" while the latter "seems to have arisen in reaction against the social reformist orientation" (p. 84). Where this historic divide is relevant to ethics becomes clear when asking questions about personal values, as we illustrate shortly.

Questions about the role of adult educator as social change agent can be found throughout the literature of adult education and training and have even been presented in a pro/con "debate" format at times (Beatty, 1992; Even, 1981; Healy, 1981; Ilsley, 1992). In a particularly insightful discussion, House and Cunningham debated the question, "Should educators educate or advocate?" In this exchange, House (1990) makes the point that education, persuasion, and propaganda are "mutually exclusive commodities" (p. 14). As an illustration, House states that the "objective of public policy education is to educate about a controversial issue without being controversial" (p. 16). Cunningham (1990) responds by arguing that "[n]o education is neutral" and, indeed, the "*most* dangerous teachers are the ones who say they are objective" (p. 18).

Of course, these are complex questions that usually involve much more than an either/or response. For those educators firmly ensconced in the social change camp, this belief does not pose an ethical dilemma. It can become problematic, however, when a person's actions impact on obligations to another party, or when such advocacy is presented in a way that silences those learners who may hold a different perspective on the issue. On the other hand, neutrality and objectivity are myths. The politically neutral classroom or the objective instructor simply do not exist (Colin III & Preciphs, 1991; Collard & Stalker, 1991; Gajdusek & Gillotte, 1995; Moe, 1990; Sheared & Sissel, 2001). As Cunningham (1988) has so aptly stated:

> It is only when we educators realize that we are not neutral, and that being a capable program planner is not *the* only endeavor, and that choices permeate our everyday world, that we confront our responsibility for ends as well as means. To know that *all* adult educators have choices and make decisions means that power is available to all. (p. 142)

Figure 4.1 provides several social change questions to consider when using the EDM model.

Ethical Questions Related to Advocacy for Social Change

Values	*Obligations*	*Consequences*
To what extent is my role to advocate for social change or reform? Or is my primary role to provide information and a forum for exploring differing points of view? (Cunningham, 1990; House, 1990)	To what extent am I responsible for presenting multiple viewpoints and then leaving it to the learners to come to conclusions and take action they believe is appropriate?	Do I have any sense of what possible repercussions might occur from my actions? How does this fit in relation to the likelihood that change will take place?
Is my primary responsibility as an educator to encourage learners to engage in social action or is it to help them look at social issues through various lenses so that they can make informed decisions about the actions they wish to take?	How should I respond if the issue under consideration involves taking action in opposition to the mission of the company/institution that employs me?	Could it be unethical for me to promote social change with learners who had not been concerned about an issue previously, but now face dissonance over the issue? (Horton, Kohl, & Kohl, 1990)
Should the primary mission of adult education and training be to transform society or to promote individual growth and fulfillment? (Beatty, 1992; Even, 1981; Healy, 1981; Ilsley, 1992)	Should I be willing to share my own views and biases with learners without directly encouraging them to adopt my position?	If I were to choose to *not* assume an advocacy role, especially on issues that are particularly troubling such as racism and sexism, am I selling out on my core values in a way that I cannot accept? (Sheared & Sissel, 2001)

Figure 4.1 Advocacy for social change questions to consider when using the EDM model

TECHNOLOGY

So many questions have surfaced regarding technology and ethics during the past two or three decades that we could easily write a book on this topic alone. In fact, entire college courses have been developed around the topic of technology and ethics. At the time of this writing, McCrickerd (n.d.) offers a course at Drake University entitled "Technology & Ethics." In this course she helps students develop their critical thinking, speaking, and writing skills as well as familiarizes them with contemporary discussions in technology and ethics. Mitcham (2001a), a leader in the area of technology and ethics, teaches a course that critically analyzes politics and ethics of contemporary communication technology. At Elmira College two graduate courses in adult education that deal in some way with technology ("Computer Mediated Distance Education" and "Computer Technology and the Educator of Adults") have significant components dealing with ethics (Hiemstra, 2002b).

Such difficult questions surrounding critical issues like using advanced technology to prolong the life of severely ill patients, using technological advances in space science to terraform a distant planet, or cloning prehistoric creatures from ancient DNA have so many ethical ramifications it boggles the mind of anyone reflecting critically about technology. In adult education, similarly difficult questions exist pertaining to such issues as appropriate uses of technology in the classroom, using distance learning for degree programs, and maintaining confidentiality in electronically shared student databases.

The advent and increasing popularity of the personal computer and, correspondingly, the World Wide Web have created an even larger number of ethical dilemmas. Barbour (1996) provides a systematic and comprehensive discussion of this area as he talks about the various conflicting values between technology, humans, and the world in which we all live. He also suggests that a combination of education, political action, cataclysmic crises, and communal values must come together as we work through potential or existing ethical dilemmas. Various other related issues are discussed in Shrader-Frechette and Westra (1997).

Mitcham (2000, 2001b) believes technology is actually in the process of metamorphosing into a post or hyper-technology era. He notes:

> From mainframe through personal computer to Internet the electronic computer has transformed information and human communication in unanticipated ways that are giving birth to what has been variously termed cyberspace, virtual reality, or hyperreality. To live in this new milieu, which transforms not just calculations and communications but the sense of body, self, and culture, it is not clear that ethics in any traditional sense (as that which emerges from place specific ethos) is possible. (Mitcham, 2001a, ¶ 1).

Baird, Ramsower, and Rosenbaum (2000), Ermann (1997), Holt (1998), Johnson (2000), and Johnson and Nissenbaum (1995) are only a few among many others who provide further information on this topic.

Some scholars have suggested we need ethical statements that provide clearly developed values and guidelines steering the utilization of any form of technology within an educational setting. Correspondingly, Barquin (1992) notes that the Computer Ethics Institute developed a statement pertaining to computer ethics. Beverly (1993) developed an ethical statement related to technology in education that covers such topics as human values, human responsibility, confidentiality and privacy, and technological acquisition. While such recommendations exist, we believe the EDM model can serve as one mechanism for educators and trainers of adults to work through dilemmas or issues that arise from topics associated with technology. Figure 4.2 provides technology-related questions to consider when using the EDM model.

CENSORSHIP

Very little has been written about censorship in adult education. Yet we know it exists, in both overt and covert ways. For those educators committed to the free exchange of ideas, cen-

Ethical Questions Related to Technology

Values	*Obligations*	*Consequences*
To what extent is it my role to promote adherence to the highest ethical standards in terms of technology? Or is it my role simply to serve as a role model, such as not allowing software piracy to take place within my organization? (Software Publishers Association, 2002)	How should I ensure that learners respect the words and ideas of others because of the ease with which digitized information can be manipulated and even stolen? (Holt, 1998)	How can various distance education approaches and the growing pervasiveness of the Internet can be used to facilitate hegemonic control over information? (Holt, 1998)
Is it my responsibility as an educator to ensure that a situation of "haves" vs. "havenots" does not limit access to an educational resource for certain learners? Does my responsibility include adequate training of all learners in using technology? (Grill, 1999; Holt, 1998; Lovell, 1993; Nelms, 1993)	How should I respond if institutional or organizational constraints or policy continue to limit access because of technological adoptions? (Hickman, 1999; Hopey & Ginsburg, 1996)	Do I really understand the ramifications of any limits to access? Can I change my use of technology to improve access? Are there related staff development and teacher training that I can implement to improve access? (Baird, 1995; Gibson & Gibson, 1995; Grill, 1999; Hopey & Ginsburg, 1996)

Figure 4.2 Technology-related questions to consider when using the EDM model

Values	*Obligations*	*Consequences*
How do I answer to critics who say the use of technology can be dehumaniz-ing and even sterile or socially isolat-ing? (Rose, 1993)	How can I incor-porate human inter-activity in any virtual classroom for which I have responsibility in a way that promotes optimal learner in-volvement? (Bulik & Hanor, 2000; Hopey & Ginsburg, 1996)	How do we train learners in the ef-fective use of tech-nology to ensure satisfying human interaction, learner control options, and critical reflection op-portunities? How do we ensure that good instructional design is used to permit person-to-person involve-ment? (Bulik & Hanor, 2000; Rose, 1993)

Figure 4.2 Technology-related questions to consider when using the EDM model (*continued*)

sorship clearly poses an ethical dilemma. Frequently, when we think of censorship, we are reminded of cases where public schools are asked to remove (or not include) certain materials from their libraries. Classic works such as *Huckleberry Finn*, *Catcher in the Rye*, *The Grapes of Wrath*, and even Anne Frank's *Diary of a Young Girl* have been challenged. These cases are documented and reported annually by the First Amendment ad-vocacy organization, People for the American Way (2002).

We believe that censorship qualifies as a common concern for educators and trainers of adults for several reasons. First, one of the hallmarks on which the adult education movement has been founded is the free exchange of ideas. This notion is associated with the influence of progressive philosophy, and is perhaps most readily identified in the ideas of Eduard Lindeman (1989). Examples from the history of adult education include the public forums movement (Boggs, 1986), the Center for the Study of Liberal Education for Adults (Knox, 1962), and High-lander (Adams, 1975).

Second, adult education has a clear link to culture and cultural institutions. Many of the battles over censorship are played out in museums, libraries, and the media. The Internet has even taken this issue to a whole different dimension. Cultural institutions such as these are important locations for adult learning, and so any attempt to restrict access to ideas and information has clear ethical implications.

Third, as a field, we have tended to overlook the possibility that censorship exists within our own practice. A continuing education program planner who chooses to not offer a course because of its New Age content, who decides to not invite certain speakers with controversial ideas to make a presentation, or who imposes a predetermined curriculum from which instructors are admonished not to deviate—all these smack of censorship. For example, several years ago Ralph was told of an incident where the community education program of a school district decided to offer a course on shamanism. A small local group of two or three individuals challenged the course on grounds that the group would be practicing religion. Eventually, fearing a possible lawsuit, the decision was made to withdraw the course, which actually wound up being offered by the instructors on their own at a local church.

Fourth, and perhaps most relevant to a discussion of ethics, opposing censorship often requires courage and a clear sense of personal values. To truly believe in the free exchange of ideas means being willing to accept that *all* views should be allowed to be aired, no matter how personally distasteful or even repulsive. People who view censorship as unethical will find themselves "defending" the rights (not necessarily the ideas) of racists who distribute pamphlets in a public place, pornographers who publish magazines, and certain kinds of music with lyrics that may be personally offensive. Of course, these examples are extremes, and are not likely to be a factor in training and education situations. However, they show how educators who desire consistency in opposing censorship can be thrust into supporting the right to *present* ideas and materials that they vehemently oppose on a personal level. Figure 4.3 provides questions relative to censorship you could consider when using the EDM model.

Ethical Questions Related to Censorship

Values	*Obligations*	*Consequences*
How often do I censor myself when teaching by avoiding ideas I do not personally agree with?	To what extent do I have a responsibility to present differing sides of an issue or idea to learners, even when some of those perspectives will be controversial? (University of Southern Mississippi, 2000)	Am I willing to recognize and accept the *entire* spectrum of consequences possible for supporting the free exchange of ideas? (People for the American Way, 2002)
Do I believe that it is appropriate in some situations to place restrictions on the kinds of teaching methods and materials instructors are permitted to use? (Marsh, 1991)	Is it my responsibility to serve my institution by upholding certain standards of decency as an instructor?	How would I respond if I were not allowed to present certain material in my classes or to offer courses on topics in my field that some would consider unpopular or inappropriate?
Do I believe that being able to share ideas freely outweighs the possibility that some ideas will be offensive or potentially disruptive to some learners? (National Coalition Against Censorship, n.d.)	To what extent do I have a responsibility to students to share all ideas, including some with which I personally disagree?	Do I believe it is appropriate to limit or avoid certain topics, speakers, or instructors because they may be controversial and/or bring negative publicity to my institution, business, or program? (American Library Association, 2002)

Figure 4.3 Censorship-related questions to consider when using the EDM model

MARKETING

The ethical considerations underlying the way any organization promotes its services or products today must be front and center in the minds of top leaders. As Brennan (1998) notes, "The consumer movement and the environmental lobby are now firmly established as vigilant and powerful watchdogs" (p. 8). In fact, many organizations have responded to such pressures and corresponding criticism with a more consumer-oriented approach to the way business is done and goods and services are mandated.

Marketing is also a necessary function for the success of most adult education programs. In essence, if prospective clients, students, or participants do not hear, read, or know about what is available, they will miss out on a potentially ideal learning opportunities. However, there are many inherent ethical dilemmas or conflict possibilities within the design and implementation of any marketing strategy, including adult education marketing efforts.

As with the area of technology, several institutions of higher education offer courses that deal in some way with marketing ethics. For example, New Mexico State University offers a graduate course entitled "Business Marketing Ethics" where students are exposed to ethical argumentation methods and encouraged to examine various ethical issues related to marketing (Hyman, 1996). Boston College has a graduate course entitled "Marketing Ethics and Creative Thinking" where students are helped to apply ethical reasoning to ethics in business and in marketing (Keyes, 2002). In Elmira College's Graduate Adult Education Program, a course entitled "Administration in Adult Education Organizations" has a unit on legal and ethical issues as they relate to marketing within administrative decision making (Burns, 2000). The textbook for the course (Galbraith, Sisco, & Guglielmino, 1997) contains considerable material related to marketing and ethics.

One of the dilemmas foundational to possible ethical conflicts in marketing any type of program or service is related to a need for competition. Thus, we see such metaphors as strategy, tactics, competitors, and targets used as the language in many advertising materials. These terms often emphasize notions of power, control, and dominance, which can be seen as the antithesis of various concepts foundational to adult education such as concern, caring, cooperation, and humanism (Brockett, 1997). It is difficult to think positively about moral or ethical behavior when seeking power or control. Paradoxically, the marketing concept itself can add to a risk for unethical behavior because of motives such as profit, course cancellations with low enrollments, and less than accurate descriptions of offerings or services.

In reality, most examples of unethical conduct pertaining to marketing that make the headlines are those where some teacher, trainer, or administrator knowingly or intentionally tries to deceive a learner in some way. For instance, a course may be advertised at a certain fee with an implicit assumption described in the write-up that there is a break even amount based on a minimum number of enrollments. However, as Sork (1988) notes, if a programmer employs a Robin Hood principle, in which a charge is actually increased by a certain percentage so other programs or courses can be subsidized in some way, an ethical dilemma can be created. On the other hand, Solomon (1992) reminds us there is a financial value associated with risk that can be justified as added costs to final product financial requirements. Employing the EDM model can help program administrators sort through their decision making on such issues. Figure 4.4 provides questions related to marketing that may help you in the sorting process when using the EDM model.

SELF-DIRECTED LEARNING

Self-directed learning as a concept, process, and even learning style or approach has received considerable attention in the three to four decades following the groundbreaking research of Houle (1961) and Tough (1979). Like any new idea, though, supportive literature, controversy, and even condemnation have followed in its wake. The International Self-Directed Learning

Ethical Questions Related to Marketing

Values	Obligations	Consequences
To what extent is it my role to describe all benefits that are available to adult learners participating in an educational program? (Burns & Roche, 1988)	Is it my obligation to describe to learners any disadvantages, limitations, or problems associated with participation in an educational program? (House, 1996b; Zinn, 1993)	Do I fully understand both the advantages and disadvantages for learners involved in an educational program who expect certain outcomes? Are there unknown repercussions in not understanding? (Clement, Pinto, & Walker, 1988; McDonald & Wood, 1993)
What do I value in terms of truth in advertising versus the need my institution has to not lose money in an educational program? (Preston, 1996)	Is it my obligation to ensure that all advertising materials for an educational course or program include only truthful information and that they do not promise more than can be realistically achieved? (Price, 1997)	If I choose to not include all relevant information about a program, do I make myself liable to learners in some way in either a moral or legal sense? (Lawler, 1996)
To what extent should particular clients be involved in any aspect of planning programs, including marketing? (Sork, 1997)	Do I have an obligation to seek out input from representative learners who may be impacted by my marketing strategies? (Wilson & Cervero, 1996)	Do I understand how issues of what is right or wrong for learners stand in potential conflict with published institutional codes or guidelines? (Lawler & King, 2000)

Figure 4.4 Marketing-related questions to consider when using the EDM model

Symposium, held annually since 1986, has brought worldwide attention to the concept and helped build the positive image prevalent today in the minds of many people involved with the education and training of adults (Durr, 2002; Long & Associates, 2000). At the 1996 Symposium, we raised a number of questions relative to ethics and self-direction (Brockett & Hiemstra, 1996).

The potential for ethical conflict exists in various ways. For instance, one of self-directed learning's central precepts is helping learners take personal responsibility for their own learning (Hiemstra, 1994). By being able to select personal objectives, learning resources, time lines, and evaluation strategies, many adults can be helped to be more efficient and effective as learners. However, an ethical dilemma arises when it is assumed that efficiency or effectiveness and self-direction are always linked and, indeed, desired.

Consider the example of different ways of approaching genealogical research. Roger has developed a large database about the Hiemstra name going back to the early 1500s in Holland. He has done this in a fairly self-directed, systematic way starting from an initial course on genealogy techniques, followed by lots of reading, self-study, trips to Holland, and many hours reading old records. A third cousin of his, on the other hand, has compiled a fairly similar record mainly through correspondence or face-to-face discussions with his various relatives. When they met and compared databases, Roger found some errors in the cousin's records due most likely to oral histories changing over time. However, he observed the pride and enjoyment obvious in the cousin's work and resisted suggesting procedural changes that could have enhanced effectiveness and accuracy, but perhaps reduced the pure enjoyment possible from personal contacts with living relatives.

Another potential ethical conflict can stem from educators or trainers who employ self-directed learning approaches inappropriately or with little understanding of a learner's readiness for self-direction. Any teacher or trainer who insists each learner engage in self-directed learning activity without determining individual readiness, perceptions about the process, study skills, information acquisition abilities, and expectations about student or teacher roles is creating a possible ethical conflict. We believe that facilitating such learning is demanding, complex, and dependent on understanding as much as possible about the adult learner. As we have said elsewhere, "a facilitator of self-directed learning must get to know each learner and be able to help them to develop and explore personal interest areas. . . . there is a very fine line between promoting self-direction and non-direction. We believe the facilitator of self-directed learning needs to assume a proactive role in working with learners" (Brockett & Hiemstra, 1991, p. 202). There is much that can be lost in the teaching-learning process if this is not done and, ethically, we believe each teacher or trainer is obligated to do so. We suggest the EDM model is a useful tool for thinking through such ethical dilemmas and raising questions of value in determining solutions or answers. Figure 4.5 provides several related questions.

WHERE DO WE GO FROM HERE?

A broad profession like adult education has many areas or issues of common concern that have ethical ramifications. We have presented five such concerns to demonstrate how the EDM model can be used as a vehicle for raising questions and sorting through various decisions that may be possible when confronting ethical issues or dilemmas. However, our efforts only scratch the surface of what confronts professionals throughout their careers. Such issues as the following are obvious additions to our list: (1) How should adults be taught or trained? (2) How can educators or trainers of adults better articulate programs and efforts with educators of youth? (3) How do you deal with such problems as racism, sexism, ageism, and other forms of oppressive behavior? (4) How do you provide adequate education and services to adults with disabilities? (5) Can mandatory continuing education and training programs remain true to basic tenets of good adult education practice?

What are the ethical issues or dilemmas that you most

Ethical Questions Related to Self-directed Learning

Values	*Obligations*	*Consequences*
What do I value in relation to a person's potential to accept increasing responsibility for personal learning versus determining readiness for self-direction? (Hiemstra & Sisco, 1990)	To what extent is it my responsibility to ensure that all learners have adequate preparation for lifelong or self-directed learning? (Bouchard, 1998; Hiemstra, 2002a) Do I have a corresponding obligation to help learners increase their critical reflection skills when engaged in self-directed learning? (Crowe, 2000)	Am I prepared to accept that there may be learners who are not willing, capable, or ready to be self-directed? (Hiemstra & Sisco, 1990)
How committed am I to implementing self-directed learning tools or approaches that may conflict with existing academic policies and procedures? (Brockett & Hiemstra, 1991)	To whom am I most responsible, the self-directed learner or the academic institution in which I am employed? How do I help learners negotiate their way through corresponding ethical dilemmas created by bureaucratic barriers? (Kasworm, 1992)	How consistent are my use of selected self-directed learning approaches with my personal philosophy and values as an educator? (Hammond & Collins, 1991; Hiemstra, 1988)
What do I value as an educator who believes in self-directed learning but wishes not to be seen as using self-directed approaches as an "easy" way of working with learners? (Brockett & Hiemstra, 1991)	Is it my obligation to ensure that all learners with whom I work develop the attitudes, skills, and knowledge necessary to achieve their full potential? (Candy, 1991)	Am I able to help learners fully understand the rigor required to be successful as a lifelong, self-directed learner? (Hiemstra, 2002a; Piskurich, 1992)

Figure 4.5 Self-directed learning questions to consider when using the EDM model

often face? We recommend the following steps in both determining them and thinking through some of the important questions that can be raised by employing the EDM model:

1. Brainstorm with your close colleagues in staff meetings to compare notes, determine the pressing issues, and prioritize means of dealing with corresponding ethical issues.

2. Review the periodical literature, Internet resources, and popular press items to determine issues being addressed by educators and trainers.

3. Establish means whereby clients, customers, students, and others with whom you and your colleagues work can describe issues with ethical consequences they have faced. Confidentiality may be required in some instances because of the sensitive nature of the situation.

4. Engage clients, customers, or students in discussion activities designed to synergistically elicit ethical issues that need to be addressed.

5. Research possible areas of common concern and report your findings at professional meetings, staff meetings, and in the periodic literature.

6. Arrange retreats as venues where employees can spend quality, uninterrupted time discussing common areas of concern and determining some associated ethical questions.

7. Participate in on-line forums or chat rooms designed to discuss ethical concerns relevant to your professional area of interest. If such forums do not exist, consider starting one.

The process of determining ethical issues must be a continuous one. It is our hope that one outcome from our work will be the motivation among our readers to engage the EDM model in an ongoing manner. We continue in this direction with our next three chapters. Chapter 5 describes in more detail how we can use the model to respond to the ethical dilemmas and situations that face us in our daily practice. Chapter 6 establishes some guidelines for ethical practice and includes discussion on the pros and cons of establishing ethical standards and codes of ethics for the profession. Chapter 7 examines strategies for creating ethical environments.

CHAPTER 5

Responding to Ethical Dilemmas

From the previous chapters, it should be clear that we base much of our thinking on the assumptions that (1) ethical dilemmas are often much more complex than simply being questions of right and wrong or good and bad and (2) we believe that the EDM model can be used to help educators and trainers make ethical decisions. At the same time, it would be naive to think that all ethical situations can be handled the same way. Simply put, there are times when ethical dilemmas occur because values clash and a situation has arisen where there is potential for unacceptable behavior to take place. Sometimes, the problem comes about unintentionally but in other cases, a person may engage in behavior that is inappropriate, unprofessional, unethical, or even illegal.

It is in situations such as these where the EDM model can be of particular value. The model makes it possible to delineate several key aspects of any ethical dilemma. In this chapter, we show you how the EDM model can be used to help identify major elements of ethical dilemmas that can occur in your own practice. Thus, it serves as a tool for addressing such dilemmas. Before doing this, however, we begin with a personal illustration to show how an ethical dilemma can be resolved in a nonconfrontational way where everybody wins.

In the fall of 1982 Ralph had just completed his doctorate and was in his first semester as an assistant professor at Syracuse University. Roger, who was serving as program chair, had been successful in obtaining support to begin a Weekend Scholar program option and had hired Ralph in a nontenure track position. During this semester, we chose to co-teach four courses rather than offer two courses each.

Diane (not her real name) was a student in three of these classes. She attended class regularly and made contributions like most class members. Neither of us had any indication that she was unhappy until the semester was over, grades had been submitted, and she had completed the anonymous final course evaluations. However, at the bottom of each evaluation, she signed her name. From these forms it became clear that she had substantial concerns about Ralph's instruction in the three courses. Her overall ratings for Ralph were low, and she included detailed illustrations on why these low evaluations had been given. She met with Roger to discuss the situation. Roger subsequently suggested that Diane schedule a meeting with Ralph and said he would discuss the issue with Ralph as well.

So, Roger sat down with Ralph and the conversation began something like this: "You know that I have great confidence in you as a professor, and you should not take this in the wrong way, but I've been approached by a student who had some concerns about your teaching last semester." He went on to describe the "facts" of the situation and said that Diane was willing to discuss her concerns in person with Ralph.

The two met and discussed the concerns in an open, constructive way. Ralph acknowledged that many of Diane's concerns were well founded, while standing by his rationale for other areas of disagreement. The meeting ended in a positive tone and, while Ralph was certainly concerned and troubled by the evaluation, he was able to keep the situation in perspective and appreciated Diane's willingness to talk openly, especially since she was scheduled to take a class with Ralph the following semester. Taking some of the suggestions and Roger's feedback into consideration, Ralph made a few adjustments in his teaching approaches. The next semester Diane did take his course. At the end of the semester, she came to Ralph and said that she thought this class had gone much better and that she had enjoyed his teaching.

Our reason for sharing this personal example is that it shows a potentially volatile situation where each party had much to lose. Ethical issues that could have arisen in this case include violation of confidentiality and use of power in a potentially abusive way. Yet, because of how each of us chose to respond to the dilemma, it was resolved in a nonconfrontational way with everyone coming out winning. Diane was able to share her concerns openly and did so without facing retribution. Roger was able to function in a constructive mentoring role with his new colleague without being overly critical and jeopardizing a close professional and personal relationship. Ralph gained some useful feedback to help him improve his teaching in the next semester.

THE EDM MODEL WORKSHEET: A PRACTICAL TOOL FOR ANALYZING DILEMMAS

While dilemmas such as the one described above have the potential for an ideal resolution, we know there are many ethical situations that do not lend themselves to such a clean end result. In these situations it makes sense to take time to reflect on important issues and weigh key aspects, options, and possible consequences. To assist in doing this, we designed the EDM Model Worksheet (see Figure 5.1).

We repeat, however, the caveat in Chapter 2 that most often, ethical dilemmas in practice arise suddenly, with little time to reflect on or study the dilemma. In such situations where a quick response is needed, it is obviously not practical to work through a detailed process deliberately. We recognize this and remind you that the EDM model is intentionally designed to help you step back in a reflective manner and think through the process of making ethical decisions in a way that is not likely to happen in most real-life situations. Whether you do this in analyzing past decisions or as means to think through upcoming

EDM Model Worksheet

Values—What values do I hold that are relevant to the situation?
1.
2.
3.
4.

Obligations—Which obligations are in conflict in this situation?
1.
2.
3.

Consequences—What are my options and what are some potential consequences of my actions?
1. Action:
   Possible consequences
   a.
   b.
   c.
2. Action:
   Possible consequences
   a.
   b.
   c.
3. Action:
   Possible consequences
   a.
   b.
   c.

Figure 5.1 EDM Model Worksheet

decision-making situations, we believe that by doing so, it is possible to learn to think critically about ethical issues. This also will help you internalize a critical thinking approach much in the same way a musician or athlete performs in a given situation from tacit knowledge (that is, without having to consciously think about it). Thus, by internalizing the process, you eventually will be able to respond in a natural and automatic way when dilemmas do arise in your own practice.

In the following case illustrations adapted with modifications from situations we have known about or experienced, we ask you to place yourself at the center of each. Imagine yourself in the situation and think through how the information you would provide on the EDM Model Worksheet is different from or similar to what we offer. We do not prescribe an optimal response to either example, only the basic information that might allow you to make an informed decision. Later in the chapter we consider a range of possible responses to ethical dilemmas.

Case Illustration 1: Should I Stay or Should I Go?

You have been offered a position as a trainer with a local company to provide training related to cleanup of toxic waste in your community. You have questions about whether the company is truly concerned with cleanup; however, the supervisor assures you that by taking this position, you will have an opportunity to make a difference. Besides, the offer includes a good salary and benefits. So, after much reflection, you accept the position and go to work for the organization. After about a year, however, you realize that the difference you have made is minimal. You feel that by continuing to work for a company that is not acting in a way consistent with your values about the environment, you are selling out. What do you do?

Using the EDM Model Worksheet, you might come up with something as shown in Figure 5.2.

EDM Model Worksheet

***Values*—What values do I hold that are relevant to the situation?**

1. I am concerned about nuclear waste and its impact on the environment.
2. I do not feel good about working in a situation where I am not able to make a difference and may be a part of the problem.

***Obligations*—Which obligations are in conflict in this situation?**

1. To myself, as I believe that I am selling out by continuing to work for this organization.
2. To my employer, who expects me to perform according to the organization's expectations.
3. To my family, who benefits from my employment.

***Consequences*—What are my options and what are some potential consequences of my actions?**

1. **Action:** Stay and adjust to the situation; if my values are strong, maybe I can eventually have more influence.
   Possible consequences
   a. Financial security.
   b. Difficulty facing myself.
   c. Risk of not giving my best effort on the job.
2. **Action:** Raise the concerns I have with my supervisor and provide evidence to support my position.
   Possible consequences
   a. The supervisor may listen and this could eventually lead to positive action, although it has not happened during the past year.
   b. I could be labeled as a difficult employee and eventually be pushed out of the organization.
3. **Action:** Resign my position.
   Possible consequences
   a. I would be walking away from a good salary.
   b. There might be damage to my reputation, which could lead to negative repercussions when I attempt to seek new employment.
   c. I can feel good about standing by my principles.

Figure 5.2 Case Illustration 1: EDM Model Worksheet

In the real-life situation on which this example is loosely based, the person eventually chose to leave the organization. In doing so, he was criticized by some ("You just don't walk away from a job like that; you'll learn that you just don't do that") and praised by others ("This was one of the most courageous professional moves I have ever seen"). Today the person is a successful leader in his field. This example shows the range of choices available when faced with dissonance between personal values and organizational expectations. It shows that, in some cases, this gap may be perceived as so great that leaving is the only viable long-term solution.

Case Illustration 2: Conflict of Interest?

You have been invited to serve as a consultant on a three-member team charged with conducting an external evaluation for a funded project. The results of this evaluation are intended solely for project staff to make needed adjustments and improvements in the program. Because you have participated in activities sponsored by the project and have worked closely in various ways with several of the staff members, you raise the question of whether it is appropriate for you to serve in this role. You are assured that because of your previous knowledge of and experience with the program, you are in a unique position to provide feedback that will be helpful in program improvement. Also, you know that you have more personal experience with the activities of the program and, therefore, a clearer understanding than the other two consultants. Should you accept?

Figure 5.3 presents the related information.

In this instance, both parties discuss the conflict of interest question openly. The question to raise here might be something like, Is the greater good served by using an evaluator with in-depth knowledge of the project or by hiring an evaluator less familiar with the workings of the organization? Of course, it might also be asked whether the best choice might be for the program staff to conduct an internal in-house evaluation by project staff rather than hiring a team of outside consultants. This does not necessarily eliminate the conflict of interest dilemma, particularly when differing political factions may be at work within the organization. However, the internal evaluation may be more feasible in situations where the results are used strictly for in-house program improvement.

WAYS TO RESPOND TO ETHICAL DILEMMAS

Clearly, there are many possible responses to any given dilemma. In addition, we believe that there are several basic types of responses to ethical dilemmas. When deciding what course of action to take, it is crucial to think through the possible consequences of your actions. Of course it is not possible to know in advance what the outcomes will be; however, by thinking about what *could* happen, you will be in a better position to make an *informed* choice.

The responses presented in this section can be arranged loosely along a continuum from those involving less personal involvement to those involving a major personal investment. Bear in mind that some responses are more clearly relevant to situations where you are the person at the center of the dilemma, while others are targeted to situations where you may be witness to the problem and called upon to respond to the actions of others. While it is not possible for us to present all possible responses to dilemmas, the following six actions—overlooking, acceptance, persuasion, subversion, whistle-blowing, and leaving—point out how educators rarely have only one course of action available to them in any given situation. It is usually the possible *consequences* of the different responses that prove helpful in narrowing the choices and, ultimately, taking action. As you read, think about some other possible ways of responding to an ethical dilemma.

EDM Model Worksheet

Values—**What values do I hold that are relevant to the situation?**
1.   Because of my knowledge of the program, I have a perspective that would be helpful in the evaluation.
2.   As a past participant and friend to several staff members, I believe in the program and want to see it succeed.
3.   I can be fair and look at both program strengths and possible areas for improvement.

Obligations—**Which obligations are in conflict in this situation?**
1.   To myself, as I wonder if I can do this without getting in a position where I have to compromise my professional integrity, especially if I find areas that need improvement.
2.   To the program staff, as I respect them and believe in what they are doing; I wonder if I can be a part of the evaluation team without putting these people in jeopardy.
3.   To the funding agency, as it is expecting certain outcomes from the program and the evaluation team is obligated to determine whether these outcomes are being met.

Consequences—**What are my options and what are some potential consequences of my actions?**
1.   **Action:** Accept the invitation and serve as a member of the evaluation team.
      Possible consequences
      a.   My perspective on the program allows me to offer input useful to program improvement.
      b.   If the evaluation reveals serious problems, I could be placed in a difficult position and even jeopardize relationships with people I like and respect.
      c.   I could gain experience in doing program evaluation and would be compensated for doing so.

Figure 5.3 Case Illustration 2: EDM Model Worksheet

2. **Action:** Decline the invitation to serve on the evaluation team.
    Possible consequences
    a. My perspective on the program would not be incorporated into the program's evaluation.
    b. I could feel as if I am letting down people whose work I believe in and respect.

3. **Action:** Decline the invitation to participate and recommend someone else to serve on the evaluation team.
    Possible consequences
    a. I could recommend someone who shares my values about this kind of program.
    b. I would miss a potentially valuable learning experience.
    c. I would lose the consulting fee.

Figure 5.3 Case Illustration 2: EDM Model Worksheet (*continued*)

Overlooking

Under many circumstances, the idea of simply overlooking behavior that may be inappropriate seems distasteful, passive, and, in fact, inconsistent with the EDM model. As such, it generally runs contrary to our entire purpose in writing this book. However, ethical situations can sometimes arise out of unsubstantiated rumor or gossip. For example, most of us have heard stories of sexual relationships between instructors and students or between supervisors and staff members. Yet, in the majority of cases, such liaisons are discreet and thus, there is no direct evidence of unethical behavior. The risk in responding to situations for which no clear evidence exists is that it reinforces the moral nightstick approach to ethics we believe counterproductive to creating an ethical environment (in Chapter 7 we discuss strategies for creating an ethical environment). Thus, while we may personally be troubled by what we have reason to believe is inappropriate behavior by others, the possible negative consequences of making accusations based on hearsay could very easily outweigh the benefits of doing so. Remember, too, that in a setting where a nonconfrontational approach to ethics is in operation, it may be possible to raise such issues in a general, non-threatening way that lets colleagues know there is an awareness of possible wrongdoing, while not specifically pointing fingers. Sometimes, this subtle peer pressure may be enough to persuade a person to rethink questionable conduct.

At the same time, overlooking or ignoring unethical behaviors can have serious consequences. For example, overlooking unethical behavior was likely a contributing factor in the scandals that have destroyed several major U.S. corporations early in the 21st century. Historically, looking the other way played a big part in giving rise to the Holocaust and continues to play a role in serious human rights violations worldwide. The point is that there comes a time when a problem can no longer be ignored. Sometimes, the consequences of inaction can be devastating.

Acceptance

Another response to a dilemma is to accept the situation and comply with the decision, even though you may continue to disagree with it. In a situation such as the first case illustration above, some educators might conclude that the optimal response is simply to "accept and comply." A single parent in a tight job market may well decide that the greatest good is served by going along and continuing to remain employed by the organization, even though doing so is personally troubling. Here, a good litmus test is the question, "Can I still look at myself in the mirror?" or, as Blanchard and Peale (1988) ask, "How would I feel if the decision was published in the newspaper?" All of us face times in our practice when we feel that our learners, colleagues, or even ourselves have been slighted in some way. Yet, it is quixotic to think that every such situation deserves to be treated as a full-blown dilemma. Indeed, there are certain times when the greatest good may actually be served by accepting a decision, going on to other things, and saving your energy to focus on larger dilemmas that may arise.

Persuasion

Sometimes it is possible to make a case and help persuade others to rethink their actions or decisions. This response is probably most appropriate in situations where you can present evidence or data to support your position. An example would be when the director of a program designed to provide support services to economically disadvantaged community college students uses data about program outcomes to persuade senior administrators to rethink their decision to close a program because of cost-cutting measures. If the director can show that the program is serving a need consistent with the community college mission and, furthermore, can demonstrate it has contributed to an increased retention rate among the target population, then that director is acting in an ethically responsible way. When attempting to resolve an ethical dilemma through this strategy, it is important to be aware of the complex network of obligations that may exist and the various stakeholders whose values can differ considerably. But if the organization is one that nurtures a climate of trust and openness conducive to ethical practice, then perhaps persuasion strategies will encourage dialogue, discussion, and even debate as part of the decision making.

Subversion

Subversion is perhaps the most difficult and potentially troubling of the six responses. The idea of subverting policies and procedures in order to act in an ethical manner may seem at first glance to be counterproductive. Certainly it has great potential for negative consequences. Indeed, there are many situations where the act of subversion, in and of itself, may be ethically questionable. Think about a corporate trainer who is asked by a group of employees to develop and present a training program on empowering workers, a topic that management has clearly opposed in the past. If the trainer is convinced that the greatest good will be served by helping employees gain a degree of control over their work environment and work lives, then the right thing may be helping those workers develop the necessary skills. A similar situation may be experienced by an adult basic education instructor who teaches by exploring controversial topics and using reading materials that may draw disapproval from the program director. Still another example is the college professor who sometimes deviates from school policy in order to accommodate special needs of a learner such as allowing a student who does not have the money to enroll in a given semester to attend a class during that term but register for it as an "Independent Study" in the following semester.

The obvious difficulty with this response is that there is a fine line to walk if acting on behalf of learners means going directly against employer policies. Practically speaking, probably the majority of adult educators and trainers sometimes dance around strict interpretation of policies in order to accommodate learners with special circumstances. Indeed, we believe that this is often part of how educators can best respond to the needs of adult learners. At the same time, whether intentionally or inadvertently, it can be easy to cross the line and, by doing so, violate one's obligation to the employer. Because it is not possible for us to know what the fine line is in any given situation and because of the potential for serious consequences (including termination), we stress that we do not necessarily *advocate* this response in any given situation. However, we recognize that it is a possible response and, in certain circumstances, may be an option that you will find yourself considering.

Whistle-blowing

"Whistle-blowing" is one of those terms that conjures up an emotional response for many people. Some view whistle-blowers as "squealers" who should be ostracized by their colleagues and employers. Yet, reporting possible unethical activities to a higher authority, despite the possibility of dire consequences from one's actions, can be argued to be the pinnacle of ethical practice. Morgan and Reynolds (1997) mention the proliferation of popular films in the past couple of decades that exemplify this point, including film adaptations of true stories such as *Silkwood, All the President's Men, Quiz Show, Serpico,* and *Marie,* and the fictional *The China Syndrome.* In each of these stories, those who came forward to report unethical practices faced psychological and physical threats and, in the case of Karen Silkwood, her actions ultimately led to her death.

Sometimes these situations can hit close to home and affect the lives of people we know and work with. Several years ago, one of Ralph's graduate students was involved in an incident where she had reported inappropriate practices at the nuclear power facility where she worked. She did so under the belief that her report was confidential and her identity would not be revealed to the employer. When this turned out not to be the case, she was subjected to considerable harassment that had a major impact on both her professional and personal life. A documentary of her story, along with the stories of several others who found themselves at odds with the Nuclear Regulatory Commission, was produced and broadcast by CNN in the mid-1990s ("Regulation or Intimidation: Inside the NRC"). The eventual outcome included a court settlement for the individual, but also termination of her employment.

We believe that whistle-blowing is certainly a viable response to ethical dilemmas when other means of resolution are not possible or likely. At the same time, whistle-blowing can have long-term negative consequences for all parties involved. As Morgan and Reynolds (1997) point out, "[t]he wholesale adoption of formalized whistle-blowing procedures can cause serious problems in a company . . . The best-run—and most 'ethical'—corporations generally depend upon organizational trust and informal systems of communication" (p. 114). These authors stress that formalized whistle-blowing procedures can undermine trust and open communication. Again, all things considered, we encourage educators and trainers to work toward creating a climate where ethical practice is the norm and potential ethical issues are discussed openly without threat of reprisal. In the alternative, however, whistle-blowing may be necessary in order to resolve some of the more serious ethical dilemmas.

Leaving

Along with whistle-blowing, deciding to leave an organization is perhaps the most extreme response to an ethical dilemma. Here, the obvious negative consequences of lost income and uncertainty about the future can combine with less obvious consequences such as potential risk to one's reputation as a loyal employee. Yet in situations where other courses of action have proven unsuccessful and the gap between the values of the individual and those of the organization is impossibly wide, leaving may be the last—and best—option.

One way to minimize the likelihood that you will find yourself in a situation where leaving becomes the optimal response is to understand as best as possible the policies and practices of an organization *before* accepting a position. Of course, this is not often as easy as it may sound. In case illustration 1, the person had carefully checked out the organization and openly discussed his concerns during the interview. However, he was given the impression that were he to take the position, he would be able to play a role in making a difference. In other situations, such as where there is covert discrimination on the basis of gender, race, or lifestyle, a person may come to recognize this discrimination only after working in an organization for a period of time.

Which Approach?

Once again, we restate that these are but a few possible options. Furthermore, we are not advocating one response over another in any given situation. Instead we are trying to help you become better able to identify the range of responses that you might consider in a particular ethical dilemma. The key point here is that in a given ethical dilemma, you *do* have choices in how to respond. Each choice carries consequences, both positive and negative. By engaging in reflective practice (for example, Peters, 1991), it is up to you to think through possible outcomes and, based on this insight, choose the response that is most consistent with your values, fulfills the most significant or greatest number of obligations, and is likely to have the most positive consequences along with the fewest negative consequences.

EXERCISE: WORKING THROUGH A PERSONAL ETHICAL DILEMMA

Now that you have had a chance to see how the EDM model can be used to play out some examples of ethical dilemmas, it is time for you to employ it. First, make a copy of Figure 5.1 and enlarge it to a full-size page or create your own template of the figure.

Next, with a blank sheet of paper in front of you, think back on a time in your own experience as an adult educator or trainer when you faced a situation where there was ethical conflict (perceived or real). If no example quickly comes to mind, or if you have not previously worked in an adult education or training position, think of an example from your experience as an adult learner. In one page or less, write down a brief narrative of the dilemma, including its "facts," the feelings involved, and the eventual outcome.

Finally, go to the EDM Model Worksheet (Figure 5.1). Reflecting on your case illustration, take a few minutes to complete the sheet. Remember that the actual number of values, obligations, and actions that you identify may be different from the numbers on the worksheet. Simply write down all that come to mind.

As you look at the information, do you gain any insights that were not there when you actually faced the situation? Were you able to identify the core values that made the situation a dilemma for you? Do the obligations to different stakeholders accentuate the nature of the dilemma? As you look at the actions and consequences, did you list any actions that you did not consider when actually facing the dilemma? The idea here is not to get you to second guess something that you did in the past;

rather it is to show that there are often several factors contributing to an ethical dilemma and a number of considerations that might easily be overlooked.

In working through this process, it should become apparent that there are always choices to be considered. The person who says, "It's the only option I have" is actually saying, "This is the only option for which I can accept the possible consequences."

We encourage you to gain experience with the EDM Model Worksheet by thinking through other dilemmas you might have faced or are aware of from colleagues. The next time you are faced with a dilemma, why not use the worksheet to help you think the problem through? We recognize that as a busy practitioner you may find it hard to find time to engage in this kind of critical reflection. However, we are confident that the benefits from doing so will pay off for you in the long run.

WHAT CAN IT DO FOR YOU?

The EDM model is intended to help educators and trainers of adults think through specific ethical dilemmas that arise in practice. It is not a prescriptive approach in that it will not provide you with the "right" answer to your dilemma. This was never our intention. However, we hope that the EDM model helps you become better able to make informed choices relative to ethical practice based on several relevant sources of information.

In this chapter, we have described some scenarios of practical ethical dilemmas and used the EDM model as a filter through which to analyze the relevant information. By doing so, we hope that you have been able to discover the utility of this approach as a way of demystifying and destigmatizing ethical practice.

CHAPTER 6

Codes and Standards for Ethical Practice

The focus of this book has been on how individuals make ethical decisions. In Chapter 5 we provided some case illustrations and urged you to use your own experiences in working though the EDM model as a filtering mechanism for making ethical decisions. We believe that having a model to guide your thinking regarding the various dilemmas you face from day to day is a valuable tool. It helps you develop consistency in responding to such dilemmas, and will soon become a part of your daily practice. In essence, as Schwartz (1965) suggests, trying something new or different in a consistent manner over a 30-day period will form it into a habit.

Even though the book's main focus is on how individuals make decisions pertaining to ethics, it is important to recognize that ethics operates on a larger scale, too, such as within departments, units, organizations, and, indeed, the profession itself. Thus, in this chapter we look at the bigger picture by considering how formalized codes and standards might or might not contribute to ethical practice. For example, your organization or a professional association may have a published code of ethics that all employees or members are expected to follow. Even though you may be asked to use such a code as a guide for your decision making, we anticipate that the EDM model can be a useful supplement, especially as you work to integrate your own ethical standards into an organizational code or set of standards.

We begin with a brief look at some codes and standards that have been developed in adult education and training. We then identify several elements or components that such codes have in common. If you are being asked to adhere to a particular code within your organization or association, it might be helpful to compare it with some of these common elements. Next, we consider whether or not there should be a code of ethics for adult educators and discuss some of the associated debate that has taken place around this controversy. Finally, we anticipate that many readers will have affiliations with organizations that either do not have a published code of ethics or have one that is difficult to work with. So, we present some ideas on ways to articulate guidelines for ethical practice within an organization that does not rely on formally established codes and offer suggestions on how to integrate your own personal code within a larger structure.

CODIFYING ETHICAL PRACTICE

As adult education and training have developed in the United States during the past several decades there have been various attempts to professionalize such efforts. This has involved identifying some of the characteristics that pertain to professionalization (Cervero, 1988, 1992; Curry, Wergin, & Associates, 1993; Houle, 1980). Often linked to this is an attempt to codify those standards or principles determined to constitute "good" practice.

Over the past two decades or so, there have been several efforts to provide codes or standards to guide aspects of practice. For example, the Council on the Continuing Education Unit (1984) developed a set of principles aimed at promoting good practice among continuing educators pertaining to such areas as assessing needs, developing learning experiences, evaluating outcomes, and even administering programs. Although the principles were not specifically aimed at ethical issues, they provide a useful backdrop for describing the difficulties of developing guidelines that will work across the complexities of varied adult education programs and practices. Carlson (1988) and Mezirow (1984) are among several people who became concerned about the notion that any particular organization could impose standards that would somehow fit a large number of continuing educators with varied responsibilities, expectations, and approaches to working with adults.

The Commission of Professors of Adult Education, a North American professional organization, spent several years developing *Standards for Graduate Programs in Adult Education* (Commission of Professors of Adult Education, 1986; Peters, Jarvis, & Associates, 1991). These standards were developed to guide decision making in such areas as curriculum, faculty selection, resource requirements, and desired scholarship activities. Again, although ethics was not specifically covered, the standards have served to guide graduate programs as they are either developed or enhanced. For instance, in the mid-1980s Ralph chaired a search committee to hire faculty for an adult learning research center. As the committee set criteria for the qualifications of applicants, Ralph was able to share the standards with the search committee (most of whom were from outside adult education) in order to lend creditability to his position that the individuals hired should be recognized as respected scholars in the adult education field. In the late 1990s, Roger overhauled the curriculum in an adult education masters degree program. This involved changing, deleting, and adding courses to the program. The standards were crucial in convincing the College Curriculum Committee that such changes were necessary.

Laubach Literacy Action, the United States Division of Laubach Literacy International, a group devoted to supporting volunteer literacy training programs, developed a set of national quality standards for volunteer literacy programs (Laubach Literacy Action, 1996). These standards addressed such issues as governance, program management, program operations, and volunteer development. Laubach Literacy merged with Literacy Volunteers of America in 2002 to form ProLiteracy Worldwide (Kogut, 2002). They will use the quality standards as a basis for designing new standards for the combined organization.

Another example is the Code of Ethics adopted in 1997 by the Association for Continuing Higher Education (ACHE). In

1990, "Ethical Issues" was the ACHE annual conference theme. Later, a research study was conducted to better understand ethical issues facing members and the "guiding principles useful in navigating these dilemmas" (Lawler, 2000, p. 32). A second research study focused on responses to case studies relative to issues and principles associated with these cases. Subsequently, the ACHE Board of Directors approved a code, which was then approved by the membership. This code focuses on eight areas: program quality, equity, conflict of interest, confidentiality, diversity of adult learners, impact of institutional policies and procedures, advertising, and fiscal responsibility.

A final example is the Academy of Human Resource Development's (AHRD) Standards on Ethics and Integrity (Hatcher & Aragon, 2000a, 2000b). Developed by an AHRD committee and endorsed by the board, these standards identify several principles including competence, integrity, professional responsibility, respect for people's rights and dignity, concern for others' welfare, and social responsibility. Covered in these standards are the following areas:

- Research and evaluation
- Advertising and other public statements
- Publication of work
- Privacy and confidentiality
- Teaching and facilitating
- Resolution of ethical issues and violations

The above examples are aimed at serving large segments of the profession. At the same time a number of organizations have developed standards or codes designed to guide practice for a specific agency or organization. We examined a variety of published codes of ethics, which include such varied organizations and documents as the American Association of Medical Assistants' Code of Ethics and Creed, American Association of School Administrator's Statement of Ethics for Adult and Continuing Education Administrators, the American Library Association, the American Massage Therapy Association, the Council for Exceptional Children's Code of Ethics for Educators of Persons with Exceptionalities, and the Ethics Committee of the Michigan Association for Adult and Continuing Education. The

Center for the Study of Ethics in the Professions (n.d.) has an on-line database of over 850 codes of ethics from professional societies, corporations, government, and academic institutions.

The various statements ranged from one paragraph to several pages that spelled out ethical guidelines, operational procedures for boards that deal with ethical complaints, ways of applying sanctions, and appeal procedures. From these statements we synthesized a number of common elements, components, actions, or aspirations:

- Promote a high level of competence or professionalism.
- Avoid illegal acts and uphold laws, regulations, rules, and policies.
- Protect rights to privacy and confidentiality.
- Treat others with respect, honesty, fairness, sensitivity, and dignity.
- Continually develop personal skills, knowledge, and abilities.
- Avoid sexual contact or relations with students or trainees.
- Avoid impropriety, the appearance of impropriety, or personal bias.
- Avoid conflicts of interest.
- Promote diversity.
- Believe in the potential of others.

Although these elements have been gleaned from a number of formal ethics codes or statements, they might also prove useful in developing less formal organizational guiding principles or even statements of personal values. In the next section we explore the controversy centering on the question of a universal code of ethics for adult education and training.

SHOULD THERE BE A UNIVERSAL CODE OF ETHICS FOR ADULT EDUCATION AND TRAINING?

There has been considerable discussion in adult education literature about whether or not a universal code of ethics will support ethical decision making. For example, Cunningham (1992) suggests that a code of ethics is not needed for adult and continuing education endeavors, whereas Sork and Welock (1992) argue that such codes or standards are needed if we are to improve practice through our actions and decision making. Figure 6.1 provides a summary of the various pro and con stances. The material has been gleaned from various sources, as well as from insights gained in graduate classes and presentations we have made over the past several years. Although the figure is not inclusive of all possible stances, it may serve to help you understand how there can be such differences of opinion.

When you first glance at the pro side, it may seem difficult to argue against developing a code for any field of endeavor. Kidder (1995) describes existing codes of ethics for various groups and organizations. He notes, for example, that there is a growing trend to develop ethics codes in the corporate world. He further suggests that codes of ethics written in a noncomplex, straightforward manner and stressing moral values can serve as a useful guide for future decision making by any group.

Sork and Welock (1992) go so far as to suggest that "adult education is obliged to develop a code of ethics" (p. 115). They then proceed to point out various flaws in the con arguments put forth against developing a code and note several consequences in not developing a code. They also describe some of the benefits in having a code of ethics.

Connelly and Light (1991), McDonald and Wood (1993), and Siegel (2000) also have argued that the field should develop a code of ethics. Recent research by Gordon and Sork (2001) shows that a majority of practitioners believe a code of ethics for the field of adult education is needed. Wood (1996) even builds a framework for such a code by describing nine ethical responsibilities he believes all adult educators should assume. Siegel (2000) describes ten such principles for a code of ethics.

However, as noted in the con side of Figure 6.1, there are many forceful arguments as to why the field should not have a universal code of ethics. Carlson (1988) notes the following:

> Instead of trying to institutionalize adult education with a professional code of ethics, practitioners would be better absorbed in developing their own personal values and in gaining an under-

A Universal Code of Ethics

Pros	Cons
It reduces the use of situational ethics.	Absolutes discourage individualism and may force conformity.
It provides guidelines and standards for action and decision making.	Individual interpretations of codes may result in a lack of consistency.
It heightens awareness of the importance of ethics.	Individuals can develop their own personal code of ethics.
It helps identify a common set of values.	Only a very generalized code would be applicable.
It helps identify a common set of roles.	We are too diverse to agree on a single code.
It provides a vehicle for policing and monitoring behavior within the profession.	Who would develop and enforce such a code and are codes even enforcable?
It promotes consistency in behavior.	Not all people would be able or willing to adhere to a universal code.
It promotes a sense of unity and cohesiveness.	Codes can become outdated and need to be updated regularly.
It helps the field appear more professional to others.	Who decides what is "ethical"?
It helps people new to the field have a "handle" or a link.	Many adult educators are not affiliated with formal programs, so how would it fit them?

Figure 6.1 A universal code of ethics: Pros and cons

standing of the historical and philosophical foundations of their work. (p. 174)

Cunningham (1992) goes so far as to suggest that not only the field but also any professional association should not be in the business of developing a code of ethics. Fears about an elite or one particular group dictating the behavior of others serve as a foundation for arguments against a universal code, as do concerns about how such codes would be enforced and by whom. James (1992) presents an argument against certification of adult educators that is instructive. She notes the diversity of adult education providers and the variety of roles and responsibilities undertaken by the many professionals and volunteers that make up the adult education field's administrators, tutors, trainers, and counselors. Further, she discusses the instability of professional associations and many areas of practice, such as funding for literacy programs. Regarding certification, James argues that "an integrated, systematized process is beyond the capacity of adult educators today" (p. 130). The same argument can be used against establishing an all-encompassing code of ethics for the field.

We anticipate that such debates will continue in the future. Whether or not the adult education field ever develops a universal code of ethics, we assume that organizations, professional associations, and other groups will continue to develop such codes. The next section provides some suggestions on how each individual can make ethical decisions within organizations that do or do not have published codes of ethics.

ARTICULATING GUIDELINES FOR ETHICAL PRACTICE

We conclude this chapter by describing our views pertaining to codifying ethics. Often, professional ethics is thought of in terms of published codes of ethics. While there is merit in such codes, and they have helped us look at many of the issues involved in ethical decision making, we believe that published codes represent only one dimension of ethical practice. We do not think codes of ethics at the organizational, association, or discipline level often work in the way they are intended. If they are used to help people think, to open up dialogue, and to put ethics on the front burner, then they serve a useful purpose. However, if they are used to judge or categorize people or if they are tied in some way to job-related outcomes, then we believe they quickly can become counterproductive.

We further believe there is value in moving beyond the argument of whether or not there should be a universal code of ethics for the adult education field. Instead, the real issue is that what we choose to do in our individual practice makes ethical decision making viable, workable, and meaningful.

The EDM model is intended to help individuals look at what they personally can do. It is more than buying into a set of standards or having opinions about the value of ethical codes. We are not advocating here a position of ethical relativism where anything goes in terms of ethical decision making. Rather, we urge adult educators and trainers to articulate their own guidelines for ethical practice by using the EDM model as a means for incorporating ethical decision making into their professional repertoire.

We believe there is value in each person developing an individual code of ethics. For example, Roger has created one and readily shares it with students, colleagues, and others. He also regularly teaches a full graduate course on ethics in adult education and spends some corresponding time helping students think about personal codes of ethics. For one of the course tasks, students are asked to develop such a personal code. They start by examining various codes of ethics that have been developed by others. Next everyone participates in one or more discussion sessions on developing a code of ethics so a common understanding of the various arguments and issues can be covered. Typically this involves dividing each class into two groups and asking one half to adopt a pro stance in terms of developing a code of ethics and the other half to adopt a con stance. After group members study the topic and deliberate among themselves about their stance, they engage in some form of class debate to further everyone's understanding.

Then the following questions are offered as guides for students to develop their own personal development efforts:

1. What is the value of having a code of ethics?

2. How might the information be of use to you as an adult educator?

3. How can your own personal teaching or training style be affected by a code of ethics?

4. What happens if your own code of ethics does not match up with your organization's written code of ethics or, if there is not a written code, the implicit code by which the organization operates?

Students frequently mention that the process of creating such a statement can at times be very difficult and even wrenching as they wrestle with feelings, past experiences pertaining to ethics, and even religious beliefs. However, almost universally they also talk about the exercise's positive value and how it changed their view of ethics and enhanced their own ability to think critically about ethical decision making. Hiemstra (2002b) provides a link to two examples of such personal codes of ethics.

We have come to believe that if people do the kinds of things we talk about, use a process, openly talk about ethics, and even develop personal codes of ethics, then codes and formal standards at an organizational level may be less needed. In essence, we believe that if people seriously begin to apply the EDM model and incorporate it into their professional sense of self, then ethical decision making can become a normal part of professional practice.

That is why we advocate the EDM model in this book. Keeping ethical decision making at the individual level—especially when people are helped to understand issues like values, obligations, and consequences—will do more to build commitment to and consistency in making ethical decisions than any imposed set of guidelines or standards. However, it becomes crucial to establish an environment at the organizational level that supports and even encourages such individual decision making. Chapter 7 provides some guidance on building and maintaining such an ethical environment.

CHAPTER 7

Creating an Ethical Environment

In the two previous chapters we focused on showing ways of responding to various ethical dilemmas and how formal codes and statements of standards at various levels have been used to communicate the nature of ethical practice in a particular context. However, as we argued in the debate over the merits and limits of such codes, they can obscure the real issue at hand. That is, how do we create an ongoing environment in which ethical views, awareness, and knowledge guide actual practice? In addition, how do we incorporate these into our professional repertoire?

In *Creating Environments for Effective Adult Learning* (Hiemstra, 1991), Roger asked chapter contributors to think about how educators might create effective adult learning environments in which all learners can thrive. Authors focused on psychological, social, and cultural conditions that exert a powerful influence on learners as they grow, develop, and experience change. The results and subsequent works (Hayes & Colin, 1994; Taylor & Marienau, 1995) suggest that such environments can be created and sustained, but it takes effort. They do not typically develop or evolve naturally.

The same is true in creating an environment for effective ethical decision making. In this chapter we build a framework for developing such an environment. We begin by describing why local communities, various types of organizations, and even a nation set the tone for how ethics, morality, and one's personal values are incorporated into daily living. Then we describe how an ethical environment can be established and suggest several strategies to employ in sustaining such an environment. We conclude the chapter with some examples from our own professional experiences of how this has worked successfully.

WHAT SETS THE TONE FOR ETHICAL DECISION MAKING?

Ethical decisions do not take place in a vacuum. They take place, whether deliberately thought out or made instantly, based on personal views, philosophical orientation, and expectations about the consequences of one's actions. But what is the context for these decisions? It is the accumulated socialization experienced within a family, a community, and the society in which we live.

Hiemstra (2000a) writes about linking individuals through interrelationships of family, schools, and the community. However, even defining the term *community* can be difficult. Many scholars over the years have attempted to define community. Galbraith (1990) describes the multidimensionality of community. Massey (1992) describes how changes in the world economy, including the increasing rapidity of technological change, are impacting visions of "home," "place," or "locality." Decker (1992) suggests that communities need to be where learning can take place. A whole movement has even developed around the concept of "communitarianism," which promotes an effort to restore notions of responsibility by establishing a balance between rights and responsibilities and between ideas about individuality and community.

Popularized by prominent scholars and leaders like Amitai Etzioni in his *The Spirit of Community* (1994) and his ideas about creating good communities (2000), and Hillary Rodham Clinton in *It Takes a Village* (1996), communitarianism has a number of supporters. Robert Putnam (2000), in *Bowling Alone*, takes the approach that people are turning increasingly inward because of busy lifestyles, television, changing women's roles, and the Internet. He believes we must refurbish our social capital and civically reinvent ourselves by revitalizing the beliefs of people in voluntarism, community, and our democratic structures. Don Eberly (1994) also suggests that rediscovering our civic character is vital to the renewal of a vital culture. The first president elected in this century, George W. Bush, has stressed voluntarism and its potential in solving crucial societal problems through energizing communities by proposing federal support of the work of faith-based organizations (Rosen, 2000). Even though potentially fraught with political quagmires and misunderstandings, such efforts demonstrate how the tone for ethical decisions can be established at various levels.

Many of the efforts described above can be criticized because of perceived limitations regarding how rights and responsibilities are actually balanced. Ethical questions can be raised about denying certain rights in favor of certain other ones. Hartman (1996), for example, describes this in terms of the tensions that constantly exist between individual rationality and any community's socializing power over its members: "In a good community, the interests of its participants must not be narrowly self-regarded or entirely selfless. Instead, the citizens must want what will preserve the common; in the long run the community serves their interests well in part because it shapes their interests well, within limits" (p. 185).

In essence, how do you still emphasize the rights of the individual within an expectation of finding or defining what is "best" for a community? Another way of stating this is to ask how you determine the appropriate balance of shared values between an individual and all members of a community or, as Kidder (1995) describes it "the ethics of right versus right," when the requirements of a community must be weighed against the needs of each individual within the community.

Such questions or balancing will be very difficult at times and finding the right answer, right balance, or even right tone may be detrimental to one or more people despite the best of intentions. Thus, what we attempt to do in this chapter is describe how an environment can be established whereby the rights of individuals as well as the rights of people within agencies, communities, and even beyond a community setting are all considered. In addition, such an environment can promote trust and openness where ethical issues are discussed in a "safe" way before they become problematic in a given situation.

CREATING AN ETHICAL ENVIRONMENT

One way of establishing an ethical environment is to develop and enforce a code of ethics and expect everyone affiliated in some way as a member of an organization, professional association, and/or community to adhere to such a code. This type of response was considered in the previous chapter. However, as Lawler and King (2000) note, "Ethical problems arise when we are faced with a conflict of values. Values can be personal, professional, cultural, and institutional" (p. 125). We hasten to add that it is almost impossible for any code of ethics to address the various value conflicts likely to arise whenever two or more people are together.

In essence, we believe we have made a case for creating an ethical environment that does not depend on legislated, mandated, or democratically supported codes of ethics. We suggest that there are various alternatives to formal or mandated codes that are more salient in promoting ethical behavior. For example, one of the main reasons for presenting the EDM model is to provide a mechanism for each person individually or in a group setting to work through the various questions regarding values, obligations, and consequences that need to be understood or at least acknowledged in arriving at an ethically sound decision or result. As described elsewhere in this book, we also believe that it is important to destigmatize the many tough or difficult issues related to the education and training of adults, as well as such broader human problems as suicide, death and dying, divorce, mental illness, violence, and poverty that we often face in our daily living. Addressing these complex or troublesome issues in an open, straightforward way with a sense of personal courage can help us make difficult ethical decisions, perhaps not more easily, but with a sense of purpose and accomplishment. Doing so also sets a tone or climate within which other people can operate in dealing with us.

We must note here, too, that we both approach practice from a perspective heavily steeped in a philosophy that emphasizes humanism. Humanism actually has long been a major influence on adult education and training. As early as 1926, Eduard Lindeman, an adult educator and social philosopher who was greatly influenced by Deweyian progressivism, discussed the compatibility of individual growth and social change as desirable goals by making the following observation: "Adult education will become an agency of progress if its short-time goal of self-improvement can be made compatible with a long-time, experimental but resolute policy of changing the social order" (Lindeman, 1989, p. 103). We recognize there is considerable postmodern criticism of humanism (Pearson & Podeschi, 1999), but still firmly believe that self-improvement, perhaps through the development of a strong sense of self, serves as bedrock for changing or contributing to an ethical social order. This means highlighting the strengths and potential in others, rather than creating guilt or dwelling on people's limitations.

Brockett (1997) has noted that not all adult educators have embraced the humanistic orientation. For instance, Flannery (1993) has argued that humanism is limited in its tendency to "ignore the larger influences of the society" such as being socialized into roles, social strata, "influences of group interaction on one's behavior," and issues of culture, diversity, and power (p. 110). Thus, we recognize that humanism offers only one lens through which to view ethics and ethical decision making, but believe it does not necessarily emphasize the individual at the expense of ignoring social context. For us a humanistic orientation provides a framework within which we make our suggestions for creating a social context, or environment, for ethical decision making.

In the next two sections we describe crucial framework elements and approaches necessary for creating an effective environment within which ethical decision making can thrive. First, we establish the framework by describing the importance of presenting a non-confrontational approach to ethical practice. Then we include discussion about how others can be involved in ethical decision making. We conclude by describing several specific strategies you can employ in enhancing your own ethical decision-making skills over time.

To be sure, there are many times when a decision with obvious or even unknown ethical consequences must be made instantly and employing a specific strategy or framework may not be possible or practical. However, it has been our experience that paying attention to such a framework or employing the EDM model whenever possible enhances personal skills such that ethically determined decisions become increasingly more a part of the professional repertoire.

A NONCONFRONTATIONAL APPROACH TO ETHICAL PRACTICE

The term *ethics* is often associated with notions of conflict and confrontation. This, we believe, is why there is often a stigma attached to ethics and ethical practice. In response, we suggest that a nonconfrontational approach can serve as a foundation upon which ethical decision making is carried out. This idea is based on the assumption that we as humans have a common set of shared values by which we operate: "That is, most members of the society most of the time must be willing to engage in pro-social behavior because they believe in the rightness of conducting themselves in this way, rather than because they fear public authorities" (Etzioni, 1998, p. 183).

Such a statement may best serve a democratic society and there are obvious limitations even within that setting. The hegemonic nature of various systems or groups toward women (Sheared & Sissel, 2001; Stalker, 2001; Taylor & Marienau, 1995), various minority groups (Guy, 1999; Hayes & Colin, 1994; Ross-Gordon, 1993), and even certain communities (Jones, Scanlon, & Blake, 2000) often strains or limits nonconfrontational or no fault intentions in terms of attitudes toward others. Tisdell (1993) urges that attention be given to promoting inclusivity by better understanding issues of diversity, institutional contexts, and changing societal needs. Imel (1995) recommends that the multiple perspectives, experiences, and perceptions of power relationships of all individuals be acknowledged.

There will be times when it appears difficult to establish a nonconfrontational environment. For example, almost every day the media presents material pertaining to some case of road rage (or other kind of rage), overt public hostility stemming from perceived or actual experiences with poor customer relations, or worker violence and dysfunctionality. The September 11, 2001, tragedy exacerbated feelings of rage toward others. Our "hurry-up" society has led to a lack of civility and what often appears to be a loss of logic or reason. It can appear that reason and levelheaded emotion yield to extreme emotionalism or the overt demonstration of unequal power relations. Hunter (1991, 1994) goes so far as to suggest that cultural wars exist today where large groups are divided on what were once seen as core values necessary to guide a society.

Even given many instances where it could be easiest to give in to pessimism, cynicism, or despair, we firmly believe that it is possible to establish a nonconfrontational approach to dealing with others, thinking through ethical issues, and using the EDM model. We further believe such a setting can be established where inclusivity and power-sharing attitudes are the rule rather than the exception. Here we believe it is crucial that ethics not be used as a moral nightstick held over others or used against them, because the term itself can have a negative ring regardless of how much inclusiveness and power sharing are stressed. Simply asking questions about or mentioning ethics can raise issues in some people's minds of an associated stigma, sleaziness, or negativism. Unfortunately, the media's propensity to associate notions about ethics with corrupt business people or unscrupulous actions by politicians, religious leaders, or entertainers gives the term a negative connotation for some. In addition, even talking about ethics may at times result in people assuming a defensive posture because they feel they are being labeled unethical.

In reality, seldom will a situation emerge where a direct

confrontational approach is required to arrest or change certain behaviors unless criminal actions are involved. More typically what really happens is that little things accumulating from day to day eventually escalate into an obvious pattern of unethical behavior. So our intent in presenting a nonconfrontational framework is to set in place a mechanism for monitoring or supporting what each of us can do on a day-to-day basis to facilitate ethical practice. The following ideas serve as a foundation for establishing an environment conducive to a nonconfrontational approach.

Right Versus Right

As we have noted in Chapter 2, Kidder (1995) urges people to make tough choices in creating an atmosphere of ethical living. Making tough choices often involves pitting one "right" value against another, so determining the "right" choice can be very difficult. Kidder described these choices in terms of such concepts as truth, individuality, and justice. He believes that understanding the dilemmas inherent in making any ethical decision helps a person determine a course of action that is manageable, based on an understanding of personal values, and built from a sense of reason rather than just from emotion.

Open Dialogue with Others about Ethics

Often we are socialized or we learn through our professional experiences to be polite, formal, and less than direct in initial conversations with people, especially if we do not know them well or are worried about stepping on toes. Yet, decisions with ethical ramifications may be required very early in such conversations. For example, you may be asked a specific question or requested to carry out some task that requires ethically sound attention. You may need to make decisions about how to respond to an exchange prior to it turning into a confrontation. As a team or small group member working on some problem, you may begin to feel uncomfortable with the way things are progressing.

It is our view that open dialogue about the ethics involved in any situation sets a tone that can help you, as well as others, realize the importance of good ethical decision making. Such dialogue can help create a climate where potential ethical problems can be addressed openly before they escalate. We go further and urge you to talk about the importance of ethics right from the beginning of a conversation or activity. Both of us, for example, find a way to talk about some aspect of ethics in almost every graduate course we teach. Students who take multiple courses with us may experience some overlapping information, but we also anticipate that they, as well as new students, develop increasing respect for and awareness of ethical decision making.

Create a Win-Win Situation

A buzzword in business and management circles during the past decade or so has been creating a win-win situation (Gitomer, 1999). We incorporate the notion here to mean treating others with respect, increasing your understanding of where others are coming from, and making compromises that are mutually acceptable. We recognize that compromise is not always the answer and creating an ethical environment may not involve any form of compromise. However, several strategies adapted from Gitomer's work can be employed so that a win-win situation is possible in arriving at ethically sound decisions. Not all are possible each time you encounter a situation involving ethical decision making, but they serve as reminders of what can be tried.

- Understand as much as you can about another person, including expectations, personal values, and past experiences.
- Think through various outcomes of your discussions or work with others, employing as many aspects of the EDM model as possible given any time constraints within which you are working.

- Do not burn bridges or paint yourself into a corner by promising undeliverables or making an irretrievable negation of others' thoughts.
- Be honorable in the way you relate to others and be sure to consider the long-term consequences as well as any short-term ones.
- Work to uncover objections others may have or obstacles they may face through good listening, skillful questioning, and clarification of what you discover.
- When appropriate, take written notes so important points or qualifying information are not trusted to memory.
- Ask others to participate in any decision making so everyone feels some ownership in what is happening.
- Approach people directly and honestly and talk openly about potential or perceived ethical situations and dilemmas.

Often you will need to include a personal understanding of how different cultural, social, racial, geographic, and religious perspectives add complexity to the process.

Understand that Personal Responsibility
Is a Two-Way Street

We have talked elsewhere about the value of helping others assume increasing responsibility for what they do as learners (Brockett & Hiemstra, 1991; Hiemstra, 1994). We believe this is also true for engaging with others in making ethical decisions. Taking responsibility for your own actions as an ethical being is an important keystone to the EDM model, and we urge you to help others heighten their own abilities to assume increasing responsibility for the decisions they make that have ethical implications. This goes along with our earlier point about talking openly with others about ethics and, in some respects, becoming advocates for the EDM model.

We hasten to add that when we talk about personal responsibility, we mean the potential that is within each of us to grow in our ability to take charge of what we do, what we think, and how we act. Unfortunately, the term *personal responsibility* has at times been misappropriated by some who use it as a rationale for blaming the victim in situations such as unemployment, welfare, poverty, and criminal behavior. Here, the rationale goes, if people took more personal responsiblity for their lives, they would not be in such circumstances. This is very different from how we use the term. This is not what we are trying to say. Instead, we use the notion of personal responsibility here to mean that each individual can take an active role in ethical decision making. Establishing an environment that encourages such growth is worth the effort.

Involve Others in Using the EDM Model

We believe it is important to involve all stakeholders in any decision that may impact them ethically in some way. This may not always be possible if there are emotional or psychological impediments as was described in one of the Chapter 3 vignettes. In such cases, involving a professional counselor or some other knowledgeable person is the best strategy. Trying to employ the EDM model by yourself and then applying any outcomes to others has the potential of creating confusion, anxiety, and hostility. We have found that a positive side benefit of openly working through such situations with others is an increased mutual respect for and acceptance of each other's views and, perhaps, even new or enhanced friendships.

SPECIFIC STRATEGIES FOR ESTABLISHING AN ETHICAL ENVIRONMENT

What can an individual or organization do to establish and maintain a nonconfrontational ethical environment? In this section we describe several specific strategies. Obviously, it is not possible or even necessary to use all the strategies each time you employ the EDM model. However, we provide a variety of strategies so you have options for finding what might work best in a given situation.

Discover Shared Values

This strategy is sometimes referred to as moral dialogues, ethics consults, achieving ethical consensus, consensus-oriented dialogue, or values-talking. It involves working together with one or more people to identify the various values or moral aspects of any situation and determine corresponding common and different perspectives. Typically it promotes a better understanding of differences and works to build on shared or overlapping values that are discovered through discussions on the relative merit of various values.

Although consensus building is an ultimate goal, arguments raised about issues should be carefully examined and even challenged when a clear understanding is not possible. Etzioni (2000) and Keller (1998) recommend that various rules or protocols be followed in carrying out such dialogue, such as agreeing not to demonize each other, refraining from depicting the values of others as negative, and respecting each other's autonomy and views.

Resolve Conflicts in Your Own Mind

There will be times when you know in your own mind that you have personal conflicts about values or moral stances you should take. The EDM Model Worksheet in Figure 5.1 provides a mechanism for recording the various values you believe are relevant to a particular situation, the associated obligations, and the possible consequences of any actions you might take. Not only can this help you develop various action possibilities, we have found that the act of writing down such information typically helps clarify thoughts in a way not possible just through thinking about it or carrying out some actions on the fly.

Use the Ethical Practices Analysis

Another strategy that might help in creating an ethical environment is to engage in the Ethical Practices Analysis presented by Sork (1990) to help practitioners examine the ethical dimensions of their work. The analysis involves the following 10 steps:

1. Decide who to involve.

2. Identify the functions to be included.

3. Specify the practices to be analyzed for each function.

4. Prepare moral arguments to justify and refute each practice.

5. Refine the arguments.

6. Discuss and debate the arguments.

7. Identify and discuss the ethical consequences of continuing, modifying, terminating, or instituting each practice.

8. Identify and discuss the practical consequences of continuing, modifying, terminating, or instituting each practice.

9. Decide which practices will be continued, modified, terminated, or instituted.

10. Prepare summary report and action plan.

As can be seen from these steps there are some clear similarities between the Sork's process and the model discussed in this book. Issues related to values, obligations, and perhaps most directly, consequences, can be found in both. The major advantage of using the analysis is that it is done collaboratively in a group setting. As such, it has the potential to complement efforts to create a nonconfrontational environment where ethical practice is alive and well.

Bring in a Third Party

As the country music singer, Kenny Rogers, once sang, "You've got to know when to hold 'em, know when to fold 'em." By this we mean there will be times when you are faced with an ethical dilemma and your personal experiences, abilities, or even legal responsibilities are not sufficient to resolve the situation. Thus, utilizing a counseling service, asking a colleague to provide some advice, or even turning to a religious professional might be the most appropriate choice you can make. As noted in the Chapter 3 vignette about the student in emotional crisis, bringing in a university counseling service was not only the correct thing to do, it also resulted in some medical help for a person badly in need of it.

Develop Your Personal Code of Ethics

As we noted in Chapter 6, we do not favor the development of codes of ethics by which large groups of people are expected to adhere. However, we do support the notion that each person is capable of developing a personal code of ethics that will serve to steer decisions regarding issues with ethical consequences. As a matter of fact, Roger in his courses urges most students to develop such a code and to periodically revisit the code to make appropriate changes as they gain new insight, experience, and responsibilities.

WHERE CAN YOU GO FROM HERE?

In this chapter we have focused on the notion that establishing an ethical environment takes the work of individuals, organizations, communities, and even a nation acting in harmony. In essence, the EDM model involves thinking about values, obligations, and consequences as broadly as possible.

Yet, it will be individuals who read this book. So what is

it that each individual can do? One obvious answer is developing and living by a personal code of ethics, and we hope our suggestions will be instrumental in helping you do so. We also hope that you will think about ways you can create an environment for ethical behavior within a broader scope. This might mean advocating ethical decision making by others through such strategies as straight talk and better understanding the values they deem as important. It also might mean conducting workshops with colleagues, community members, or others willing to enhance their ways of dealing with ethical dilemmas. In Chapter 8 we bring closure to the discussion by looking at some possible next steps.

Above all, we fervently hope that the EDM model will be a tool that becomes a natural part of each reader's professional repertoire. If sound ethical decisions are made by an increasing number of educators and trainers of adults, an environment that encourages, and even cherishes, ethical behavior can become reality.

CHAPTER 8

Ethical Practice: Some Concluding Thoughts

Those of us who work with adult learners are in a pivotal position to have an impact on their lives. Whether you work in a college or university, business, government, literacy, or community-based organization, or one of the countless other settings where adult learning takes place, the decisions you make and the actions you take can have wide-ranging impact on individuals and institutions alike.

In this book, our purpose has been to show how ethics lies at the heart of effective practice and to share some practical ideas and techniques that you can use when faced with making ethical decisions. Our focus has been largely on the individual decision-maker and how ethics touches each of our lives. Of course, ethical decision making does not occur in isolation; rather it takes place in the larger context of classes, programs, organizations, and society at large. In fact, the basic idea behind facilitating ethical practice is to improve what goes on in these different contexts. Yet, as we emphasized in the previous chapters, we see each individual educator or trainer as the *starting point* for ethical practice.

Two important areas related to an understanding of ethics are beyond the scope of our discussion, but nonetheless need to be considered for a comprehensive awareness of ethical decision making. First, there is a clear connection between law and ethics. Galbraith, Sisco, and Guglielmino (1997), in a discussion of administration in adult education, include a chapter on legal and ethical issues. As we see it, law and ethics are related but different in that law focuses on governmental or constitutional standards, while ethics is much broader. Thus, we believe ethics should be viewed on a higher standard than law. We encourage those with an interest in the relationship between law and ethics in education and training to help clarify this relationship in the future.

Second, we have only briefly touched on moral development as it relates to ethical practice. The work of scholars such as Kohlberg (1981) and Gilligan (1993) are seminal to an understanding of moral development. Kasworm (1988) has discussed ethical development as it relates to adult education by drawing from Kohlberg, Gilligan, and several other scholars. This has important implications for the values element of the EDM model that need further exploration.

It is our hope that in reading this book, you will come away with new ideas and insights. But we also hope you will raise questions and challenge some of the ideas presented here. Only through dialogue, debate, and further study is it possible to move practice forward. Clearly, ethics has moved beyond its infancy in the study and practice of adult education and training; however, the attention it has received is probably less than needed to more fully understand this perplexing dimension of practice.

We bring our examination of ethics to closure in this chapter by both looking back and looking ahead. The important points raised in the previous chapters are highlighted in the next section. Next we offer some tips for self-improvement relative to ethical decision making. This is followed by our recommendations for research needed to continue our growing understanding of ethical practice.

SEVEN POINTS WE HOPE YOU TAKE FROM THIS BOOK

Throughout the previous chapters, we presented an approach to ethical decision making we believe holds much potential for improving practice. Here, by way of summary, are seven main points contained in the earlier chapters.

First, ethics is practical. Though it is grounded in centuries of philosophical tradition, ethics is concerned with applying principles to aspects of daily living that are based on personal values and reasoning. Referred to as normative ethics, this approach can work well with both personal life and professional practice.

Second, as we presented it, ethical decision making is an individual, personal process that takes place in a larger social context. We described ethical decision making as a dynamic interaction between three basic elements that need to be considered in any ethical dilemma: (1) understanding personal values; (2) identification of the various stakeholders in any ethical decision, as well as obligations to each; and (3) assessing the range of possible choices to resolve the dilemma and anticipating possible consequences from these different actions.

Third, there is an ethical dimension to nearly every area of practice. These dimensions are found in the various roles that educators and trainers play, such as instructor, trainer, manager, evaluator, advisor, and counselor. They are also found in the many issues or controversies that revolve around how we engage in our practice. The five examples presented in Chapter 4—advocacy for social change, technology, censorship, marketing, and self-directed learning—are representative of these kinds of issues, but are by no means all-inclusive.

Fourth, the Ethical Decision-Making (EDM) model introduced in Chapter 2 and demonstrated in Chapter 5 is designed to help educators and trainers identify and reflect on real-life ethical problems. We recognize that ethical issues often arise suddenly, without warning, and require an immediate response. In such situations, there simply is not enough time to go through the steps in the EDM model. However, by taking the time to become familiar with the kinds of questions we raise, it is possible to eventually internalize the process so that you respond in a natural, almost automatic way when certain kinds of dilemmas arise.

Fifth, the philosophical beliefs each of us holds dear serve as the bedrock upon which our personal values, understandings about others, professional behaviors, and even ethical decision-making abilities develop. Fortunately, it is possible to identify, explicate, and describe such beliefs. In Chapter 3 we describe a process for developing a statement of personal philosophy and show its relationship to making ethical decisions in different areas of practice.

Sixth, codes of ethics and other kinds of formal or official standards can be helpful in identifying elements of a shared vision, especially when limited to settings such as a department or program. On the other hand, broad-ranging codes, which attempt to serve large segments of the field, seem unrealistic. Who, for example, would develop, monitor, and enforce such codes, given the diversity and fragmentation that characterize adult education and training today?

Seventh, as an alternative to the time, energy, and other resources expended on formal codes that will likely have little impact, educators and trainers of adults should turn their attention to ways of creating an environment where ethical practice is the norm. In this type of climate, it should be possible to talk about ethics in an open, honest way, where confrontation and finger pointing are minimized. We are confident that in this type of situation it is possible to address most ethical concerns early on, before they turn into potentially inappropriate or even illegal conduct. The overall value in establishing an environment for ethical decision making will be enhanced as increasingly more members of an organization incorporate such decision making into their professional practice.

TIPS FOR SELF-IMPROVEMENT

Throughout this book we have shared a wide range of tips and techniques designed to improve ethical decision making. In this section the emphasis is on the importance of self-improvement through four strategies that should help improve your ability to make more informed ethical decisions.

First, we believe in the importance of professional reading. Reading widely can help to expand your perspective about ethics and ethical decision making. It can also serve as a stimulus for critical reflection. While there is much gained from reading the adult education and training literature, we stress the importance of looking beyond this knowledge base to other professions, disciplines, and ways of thinking. For example, a number of books outside of adult education and training cited previously helped to inform our approach to ethical decision making. Among these are the works of Blanchard and Peale (1988), Etzioni (1994), Kidder (1995), MacKinnon (2001), Pojman (1995, 2001), Thompson (2000), and Weston (1997).

Other writers have provided important background for one or both of us in our own study of professional ethics. These works are not cited in earlier chapters, but we recommend them to you as helpful resources: *Consilience* (Wilson, 1998), *Ethics for the New Millennium* (Dalai Lama, 1999), *Everyday Ethics* (Halberstam, 1993), *The Ethical Decision-Making Manual for Helping Professionals* (Steinman, Richardson, & McEnroe, 1998), and *Writings on an Ethical Life* (Singer, 2000). Of course, these are but a few select books, but they proved particularly valuable to us.

Finally, we also encourage you to look to the World Wide Web in your reading and study efforts. We referenced several websites in earlier chapters and encourage you to search out others, as new resources surface regularly.

Second, we believe, too, in the power of personal and professional writing. This can range from personal journal or diary writing (English & Gillen, 2001; Progoff, 1992) to professional writing and publishing (Hiemstra & Brier, 1994). One of the best ways to learn about something is to write about it. We encourage you to write down your ideas about ethical practice and refer back to them periodically. For example, you can use the Ethical Decision-Making (EDM) Model Worksheet we introduced in Figure 5.1 to analyze dilemmas you have experienced personally or in the workplace.

Throughout this book we have used case illustrations as a way of describing ethical dilemmas. In essence, such stories bring concepts and principles to life. For example, in one of his graduate courses Ralph asks students to identify critical incidents, write down the material as a case study, and then use the

EDM model to analyze the case in terms of possible responses. We encourage you to develop case studies of your own life experiences and use them with the model, too.

Third, talking with others about what you have read or written can be very rewarding. This could entail facilitating an in-service workshop about ethical decision making within your organization, presenting a paper on the topic at a professional meeting, or something as simple as talking with a colleague or two about the whole notion of creating an environment for ethical practice in your workplace. On a larger scale, this might actually involve working to build a collaborative learning process that emphasizes the social construction of knowledge (Peters & Armstrong, 1998).

Fourth, perhaps the best way to promote ethical practice is by your own example. Modeling ethical behavior can be contagious and can contribute to the kind of ethical environment we described in the previous chapter. Of course we recognize that this view may be overly optimistic because so many different types of people with competing values work in any organization. Still, we believe modeling ethical behavior is worthwhile as some colleagues will begin to follow your example.

FROM PRACTICE TO RESEARCH

The focus of this book has been on practice. However, as a way of looking forward, we share with you some ideas about creating a research agenda on ethics in adult education and training. We title this section "From Practice to Research," because we believe that while an understanding of ethical practice has grown over the last 15 years or so, the knowledge base has lagged behind the practice. A few studies cited earlier in the book (for example, Gordon & Sork, 2001; McDonald & Wood, 1993) are more the exception than the rule.

Brockett and Kasworm (1989) wrote about the need for such an agenda, suggesting that it should be concerned with both individual and organizational aspects of ethics. They also pointed out a potential problem. Ethics can be a highly sensitive topic; thus, it is possible that respondents would be reluctant to be completely open with researchers. Those who study ethics will need to employ creative approaches to overcome problems inherent in this line of inquiry.

The following is a list of research areas or questions that we believe will be helpful in advancing our understanding of ethical practice:

- What does it mean to engage in ethical practice? Qualitative methods such as phenomenological interviewing, participant observation, and participatory research can be used to better understand how practitioners describe ethical issues that arise in their practice.
- Is it possible to create a climate for ethical practice? Action research studies of specific programs or organizations will help increase our understanding of how social context and interpersonal dynamics play a role in the way ethical issues are handled in various settings.
- Can reliable and valid instruments be developed to address psychometric properties of how or why people respond as they do to ethical dilemmas? Is it possible to examine how individuals differ on the basis of psychosocial and demographic variables? Such instrumentation and knowledge of individual differences will help us better understand attitudes and practices relative to ethical decision making.
- What does research in other fields tell us about ethical decision making? A review of the knowledge base in such fields as law, medicine, social work, and engineering might reveal some perspectives or research approaches that could serve as a framework for studying ethics in adult education and training.
- Adult educators and trainers with background and preparation in philosophical analysis can play an important role in developing further understanding of meta-analytical perspectives on ethics in adult education and training.
- It is important to understand the social context in which ethical decisions are made. How do ethical issues get resolved in different types of organizational climates?
- The EDM model can serve as a framework for studying ethi-

cal decision making. Having been developed out of practice and experience, we realize empirical evidence is now necessary to substantiate the model. Do the elements we have identified interact as we have suggested in all settings and with all types of people? Are there key elements missing from or needing refinement within the EDM model?

You may be able to suggest other directions that future research should take. There is much uncharted territory and a great potential exists for those who wish to move the study of ethics forward in the years to come.

A CLOSING THOUGHT

Our journey in studying, understanding, and applying ethical decision making reaches a new juncture with this book. It has been a period of growth and challenge for each of us. As we stated at the outset, this book was much longer in the making than either of us would have ever anticipated. Yet, what we have learned and the insights about ethical practice we have gained might not have been as rich had we not had time to interact with so many others in our graduate classes, workshops, and conference presentations.

So, for us, the journey continues. We invite you to join us on this journey and welcome the opportunity to dialogue with you as we work to foster ethical decision making in our profession.

APPENDIX

A Workshop on Creating a Statement of Personal Philosophy

Throughout our academic careers we have given our graduate students the opportunity to think about and even create a personal statement of philosophy. We have helped them understand how such philosophical beliefs and corresponding statements can serve as a foundation for ethical decision making, professional actions, and professional behaviors. In essence, we are convinced that philosophical beliefs are tied closely to ethical behaviors. For example, each of us has certain beliefs that have been shaped by such influences as cultural background and personal experiences. These have impacted on our philosophy and ethical behaviors in unique ways. If a person's philosophy is in sync with what is perceived to be the personal philosophy of one's colleagues and supervisor, it should be easier to work together. On the other hand, if these views or philosophical beliefs are in conflict, this can impact what is done or not done in the workplace and even lead to unwelcome job stress.

Thus, Roger created a workshop for developing a personal philosophy statement to help participants think through how their philosophy affects their personal style as a professional. Ralph uses a similar process in helping his students develop philosophy statements. The full workshop procedures described here can be used outside the graduate classroom, too, so you can follow them and create your own statement. Figures A.1–A.3 support the workshop and are located at the end of this appendix.

Students are provided an opportunity to undertake various experiences designed to result in the statement. Prior to the workshop they are urged to read the material by Hiemstra (1988) and Hiemstra and Brockett (1994) as background information. The workshop begins with a presentation that offers some foundational knowledge on various philosophical systems or models and that serves to elicit corresponding large group discussion. Hiemstra (2002b) depicts what such a presentation could include.

Then participants are divided into small groups to discuss various aspects of the material just covered. They utilize the following questions as discussion guides:

1. What was the message for you in the presented information?

2. How might the information be of use to you as a trainer or teacher of adults?

3. With what parts do you agree and with what parts do you disagree?

4. How is your own personal training or teaching style affected by your philosophical beliefs?

A spokesperson for each small group then reports a discussion summary to the larger group and any appropriate large-group discussion ensues.

Learners are next given an opportunity to work in dyads or triads and begin developing a personal statement of philosophy. They are encouraged to use materials distributed during the workshop as guides for initiating development of their statement (Hiemstra, 1988, 2002b) and discuss some of their initial thinking with each other. The first handout portrays several philosophical orientations or models that can be used as a personal comparison tool (Figure A.1). The second is a worksheet that can be used to guide creation of a personal statement of philosophy (Figure A.2). The purpose of this final time period is for each learner to take advantage of the synergistic possibilities in sharing thoughts and questions with each other.

The workshop concludes with a challenge to participants to each prepare a statement of personal philosophy and corresponding style related to their work with adults as learners.

They are asked to share it with classmates, work colleagues, and any other people willing to provide them with feedback on their work. They also are encouraged to examine any available statements of philosophy from other people as possible models for their own work (Figure A.3). Hiemstra (2002b) provides links to three such models.

We recommend, too, they complete the *Philosophy of Adult Education Inventory* (Zinn, 1990) during the workshop or later to acquire additional insight into how their own views match with certain philosophical models. Besides Zinn's inventory, they are encouraged to peruse Elias and Merriam (1995) if they desire additional information on various philosophical models. Typically, they are asked to submit it for instructor feedback. The workshop concludes with the suggestion that they redo their statement of philosophy every few years to reflect normal maturation as a professional.

PHILOSOPHICAL SYSTEMS AND EDUCATION

System	Component	Representative Statement
IDEALISM	**Meaning**	The overall meaning is in life itself.
	What Is Reality	Divine or absolute truths.
	Nature of Being Human	Each of us is a part of this meaning.
	Educational Aims	Tell others the truths.
	Educational Method	Inductive reasoning; authority lecturing.
	Educational Content	Life's events; the world of our own mind.
	Main Criticisms	"Truths" may be only in beholder's eyes.
	Key Proponents	Plato (Cushman, 1958; Taylor, 1926).
	Programs/ Practices	Some religious education programs.
REALISM	**Meaning**	Empirically proven facts; reality.
	What Is Reality	Natural laws and facts.
	Nature of Being Human	Awareness is perceiving.
	Educational Aims	Develop intellectual abilities.
	Educational Method	Inductive and scientific reasoning.
	Educational Content	Life's laws and principles.
	Main Criticisms	Empirical facts always subject to change.
	Key Proponents	Chisholm (1961); Whitehead (1933).
	Programs/ Practices	Phenomenology; science education.

Figure A.1 Philosophical orientations in education

PROGRESSIVISM	**Meaning**	Concrete facts and interrelationships.
	What Is Reality	Theory is based on truth.
	Nature of Being Human	Humans are part of the environment.
	Educational Aims	Development through experiencing.
	Educational Method	Problem solving; experimental method.
	Educational Content	Build on peoples' experiences and needs.
	Main Criticisms	Diminishes traditional role of teacher.
	Key Proponents	Bergevin (1967); Dewey (1938); Lindeman (1926).
	Program/ Practices	Adult basic education; community education; cooperative extension.
LIBERALISM	**Meaning**	Freedom comes through a liberated mind.
	What Is Reality	Humans endowed with the ability to reason.
	Nature of Being Human	Improvement through intellect and wisdom.
	Educational Aims	Development of the mind.
	Educational Method	Critical reading; teacher as expert.
	Educational Content	History; humanities; the classics.
	Main Criticisms	Past may not relate to modern problems.
	Key Proponents	Aristotle (Bambrough, 1963); Hutchins (1968).
	Programs/ Practices	Chautauqua; Elderhostel; Great Books; Lyceum; Center for the Study of Liberal Education for Adults (CSLEA).

Figure A.1 Philosophical orientations in education (*continued*)

BEHAVIORISM	**Meaning**	Human behavior is tied to prior conditioning.
	What Is Reality	External forces control human behavior.
	Nature of Being Human	Stimulus creates response.
	Educational Aims	Behavioral change; develop survival skills.
	Educational Method	Conditioning; feedback; practice.
	Educational Content	Basic skills; life skills.
	Main Criticisms	Learning too complex for behavior control.
	Key Proponents	Skinner (1971); Tyler (1949).
	Programs/ Practices	Adult Performance Level test; behavior modification and objectives.
HUMANISM	**Meaning**	Intellect distinguishes humans and animals.
	What Is Reality	Humans have potential and innate goodness.
	Nature of Being Human	Autonomy, dignity, and freedom are sacred.
	Educational Aims	Individual potentiality; self-actualization.
	Educational Method	Facilitation; self-direction; teamwork.
	Educational Content	Any curriculum is a vehicle for meeting needs.
	Main Criticisms	Important societal goals can be missed.
	Key Proponents	Elias/Merriam (1980); Knowles (1980); Maslow (1976); Tough (1971).
	Programs/ Practices	Individualized instructional process; learning projects; sensitivity training.

Figure A.1 Philosophical orientations in education (*continued*)

RADICALISM	**Meaning**	People create culture, history, and meaning.
	What Is Reality	Knowledge leads to understanding of reality.
	Nature of Being Human	Humans can change their environment.
	Educational Aims	Create change through education and knowledge.
	Educational Method	Dialogue and problem solving.
	Educational Content	Begin with cultural situation of learners.
	Main Criticisms	Tends to be idealistic in nature.
	Key Proponents	Adams (1975); Freire (1970); Illich (1970).
	Programs/ Practices	Community based literacy; Freire's literacy (dialectics) training; Highlander.

Figure A.1 Philosophical orientations in education (*continued*)

PERSONAL PHILOSOPHY WORKSHEET

PHILOSOPHICAL BELIEFS

My Philosophical System:

Meaning:

What Is Reality?:

Nature of Being Human:

PROFESSIONAL PRACTICE VALUES

Educational Aims:

Educational Methods:

Educational Content:

Figure A.2 Personal Philosophy Worksheet

ROGER HIEMSTRA'S PERSONAL PHILOSOPHY OF EDUCATION

PHILOSOPHICAL BELIEFS

My Philosophical System: I draw eclectically on several systems. However, the humanism model provides the foundation upon which rests most of what I do as a teacher or facilitator. I also try very hard to be consistent with the tenets of this foundation not only in what I do as a professional but also in my role as spouse, parent, friend, and community member.

Meaning: I believe that intellect is what distinguishes humans from animals and that we have the potential to expand that intellect throughout life. I also believe that there are a large number of concrete facts basic to our being able to perform as capable educational professionals.

What Is Reality?: The reality that I embrace rests on an assumption that all humans are basically good and have potential for continuous growth and development as individuals. This growth can include such features as intellectual improvement, enhanced interrelationship abilities, and expanding civic literacy skills.

Nature of Being Human: I adhere to basic humanistic notions that the dignity of each human being must be respected. I also respect each person's desire for autonomy and independence but recognize that such desire is in a constant state of fluctuation.

PROFESSIONAL PRACTICE VALUES

Educational Aims: I believe that educational aims should center on helping adults reach their maximum potential in any learning setting. This should include the development of personal intellect, the ability to think critically, and the translation of new knowledge into practical skills and behaviors.

Figure A.3 Example of a personal philosophy statement

Educational Methods: I encourage considerable self-direction and learner involvement in all aspects of a learning experience. I also use learning contracts as a means for an individual to plan a personal route through a learning experience.

Educational Content: I provide learners with some basic parameters of what the learning experience should involve or cover in order to meet professional expectations regarding the master of the subject matter. However, because there are so many ways of achieving mastery, learners are involved in some needs assessment activities at the beginning of the learning experience. This helps them plan their specific routes through the content and provides me with some input to help in my preparation of or focus for curricular material, learning activities, and learning experiences for the remainder of the course.

Figure A.3 Example of a personal philosophy statement (*continued*)

REFERENCES

Adams, F. (1975). *Unearthing seeds of fire: The idea of Highlander*. Winston-Salem, NC: John F. Blair.

Addams, J. (1930). *The second twenty years at Hull-House: September 1909 to September 1929*. New York: Macmillan.

American Library Association. (2002). *Code of ethics of the American Library Association*. Retrieved September 12, 2002, from http://www.ala.org/alaorg/oif/ethics.html

Baird, M. (1995). Training distance education instructors. *Adult Learning, 7*(1), 24–26.

Baird, R. M., Ramsower, R. M., & Rosenbaum, S. E. (Eds.). (2000). *Cyberethics: Social & moral issues in the computer age*. Amherst, NY: Prometheus Books.

Barbour, I. G. (1996). *Ethics in an age of technology: Gifford lectures volume two*. San Francisco: Harper Books.

Barquin, R. C. (2002). *In pursuit of a 'ten commandments' for computer ethics*. Washington, DC: Computer Ethics Institute. Retrieved September 12, 2002, from http://www.brook.edu/dybdocroot/its/cei/papers/Barquin_Pursuit_1992.htm

Beatty, P. T. (1992). The undeniable link: Adult and continuing education and individual change. In M. W. Galbraith & B. Sisco (Eds.), *Confronting controversies in challenging times: A call for action* (pp. 17–24). New Directions for Adult and Continuing Education (No. 54). San Francisco: Jossey-Bass.

Beverly, C. (1993). *Ethics of technology in education*. Retrieved September 14, 2002, from http://rgfn.epcc.edu/programs/trainer/ethics.html

Blanchard, K., & Peale, N. V. (1988). *The power of ethical management*. New York: Fawcett Crest.

Boggs, D. L. (1986). *Adult civic education*. Springfield, IL: Thomas.

Bouchard, P. (1998). Teaching tasks and learning tasks in a self-directed environment. In H. B. Long & Associates, *Developing para-*

digms for self-directed learning (pp. 45–62). Norman, OK: Public Managers Center, College of Education, University of Oklahoma.

Boulmetis, J. (1999). One's philosophy: How can you know you're doing it, if you don't know what "it" is? *Adult Learning, 11*(2), 2.

Brennan, M. (1998). Is there more to ethical marketing than marketing ethics? *Marketing Bulletin, 2,* 8–17.

Brockett, R. G. (Ed.). (1988a). *Ethical issues in adult education.* New York: Teachers College Press.

Brockett, R. G. (1988b). Ethics and the adult educator. In R. G. Brockett (Ed.), *Ethical issues in adult education* (pp. 1–16). New York: Teachers College Press.

Brockett, R. G. (1991). Adult education: Are we doing it ethically? *MPAEA Journal of Adult Education, 19*(1), 5–12.

Brockett, R. G. (1997). Humanism as an instructional paradigm. In C. R. Dills & A. J. Romiszowski (Eds.), *Instructional development paradigms* (pp. 246–256). Englewood Cliffs, NJ: Educational Technology Publications.

Brockett, R. G., & Hiemstra, R. (1991). *Self-direction in adult learning: Perspectives on theory, research, and practice.* New York: Routledge. Retrieved September 12, 2002, from http://www-distance.syr.edu/sdlindex.html

Brockett, R. G., & Hiemstra, R. (1996, March). *Ethical dimensions of self-direction in adult learning.* Paper presented at the 10th Annual International Self-Directed Learning Symposium, West Palm Beach, FL.

Brockett, R. G., & Hiemstra, R. (1998). Philosophical and ethical considerations. In P. S. Cookson (Ed.), *Program planning for the training and continuing education of adults: North American perspectives* (pp. 115–133). Malabar, FL: Krieger.

Brockett, R. G., & Kasworm, C. E. (1989). A framework for the study of ethical issues in adult education. *Proceedings of the 30th Annual Adult Education Research Conference.* (pp. 61–66). Madison, WI: University of Wisconsin.

Bulik, R. J., & Hanor, J. (2000). Self-directed learning in a digital age: Where next to browse is informed by reflection. In H. B. Long & Associates, *Practice & theory in self-directed learning* (pp. 265–276). Schaumburg, IL: Motorola University Press.

Burns, J. (2000). *AED 5005: Administration in adult education organizations.* Retrieved September 14, 2002, from http://www-distance.syr.edu/aed5005.html

Burns, J. H., & Roche, G. A. (1988). Marketing for adult educators:

Some ethical questions. In R. G. Brockett (Ed.), *Ethical issues in adult education* (pp. 51–63). New York: Teachers College Press.

Caffarella, R. S. (1988). Ethical dilemmas in the teaching of adults. In R. G. Brockett (Ed.), Ethical issues in adult education (pp. 103–117). New York: Teachers College Press.

Candy, P. C. (1991). *Self-direction for lifelong learning: A comprehensive guide to theory and practice.* San Francisco: Jossey-Bass.

Carlson, R. A. (1988). A code of ethics for adult educators? In R. G. Brockett (Ed.), *Ethical issues in adult education* (pp. 162–177). New York: Teachers College Press.

Center for the Study of Ethics in the Professions. (n.d.). *Codes of ethics online.* Chicago: Illinois Institute of Technology. Retrieved September 18, 2002, from http://www.iit.edu/departments/csep/PublicWWW/codes/index.html

Cervero, R. M. (1988). *Effective continuing education for professionals.* San Francisco: Jossey-Bass.

Cervero, R. M. (1992). Adult and continuing education should strive for professionalization. In M. W. Galbraith & B. R. Sisco, (Eds.), *Confronting controversies in challenging times: A call for action* (pp. 45–50). New Directions for Adult and Continuing Education (No. 54). San Francisco: Jossey-Bass.

Cervero, R. M., & Wilson, A. L. (1994). *Planning responsibly for adult education: A guide to negotiating power and interests.* San Francisco: Jossey-Bass.

Clement, R. W., Pinto, P. R., & Walker, J. W. (1978). Unethical and improper behavior by training and development professionals. *Training and Development Journal, 32*(12), 10–12.

Clinton, H. R. (1994). *It takes a village.* New York: Simon & Schuster.

Colin, S. A. J., III, & Preciphs, T. K. (1991). Perceptual patterns and the learning environment: Confronting white racism. In R. Hiemstra (Ed.), *Creating environments for effective adult learning* (pp. 61–70). New Directions for Adult and Continuing Education (No. 50). San Francisco: Jossey-Bass.

Collard, S., & Stalker, J. (1991). Women's trouble: Women, gender, and the learning environment. In R. Hiemstra (Ed.), *Creating environments for effective adult learning* (pp. 71–82). New Directions for Adult and Continuing Education (No. 50). San Francisco: Jossey-Bass.

Collins, M. (1991). *Adult education as vocation: A critical role for the adult educator.* London and New York: Routledge.

Commission of Professors of Adult Education. (1986). *Standards for graduate programs in adult education.* Washington, DC: Author and the American Association for Adult and Continuing Education.

Connelly, R. J., & Light, M. K. (1991). An interdisciplinary code of ethics for adult education. *Adult Education Quarterly, 41*, 233–240.

Cotton, W. E. (1964). The challenge confronting American adult education. *Adult Education, 14*, 80–88.

Council on the Continuing Education Unit. (1984). *Principles of good practice in continuing education.* Silver Spring, MD: Author. (ERIC Document Reproduction Service No. ED241730).

Crowe, J. L. (2000, Fall). Evaluation of adult learners: Ethical issues. *New Horizons in Adult Education, 14*(3), 4–10, Article 1. Retrieved September 14, 2002, from http://www.nova.edu/~aed/horizons/vol14n3.pdf

Cunningham, P. M. (1988). The adult educator and social responsibility. In R. G. Brockett (Ed.), *Ethical issues in adult education* (pp. 133–145). New York: Teachers College Press.

Cunningham, P. M. (1990). Own your advocacy. *Adult Learning, 2*(3), 15, 18–19, 27.

Cunningham, P. M. (1992). Adult and continuing education does not need a code of ethics. In M. W. Galbraith & B. R. Sisco (Eds.), *Confronting controversies in challenging times: A call for action* (pp. 107–113). New Directions for Adult and Continuing Education (No. 54). San Francisco: Jossey-Bass.

Curry, L., Wergin, J., & Associates. (1993). *Educating professionals: Responding to new demands for competence and accountability.* San Francisco: Jossey-Bass.

Dalia Lama, His Holiness the. (1999). *Ethics for the new millennium.* New York: Riverhead Books.

Decker, L. E. (1992). Building learning communities: The realities of educational restructuring. *Community Education Journal, 19*(3), 5–7.

Durr, R. (2002). *The 17th International Self-Directed Learning Symposium.* Retrieved September 14, 2002, from http://sdlglobal.com/

Eberly, D. E. (1994). *Restoring the good society: A new vision for politics and culture.* Grand Rapids, MI: Baker Book House.

Elias, J. L., & Merriam, S. (1995). *Philosophical foundations of adult education* (2nd ed.). Malabar, FL: Krieger.

Ellis, T. J., & McElhinney, J. H. (1992). Ethical development: An integrative model for practice. *Proceedings of the Midwest Research-to-Practice Conference.* Manhattan, KS.

Ellis, T. J., & McElhinney, J. H. (1993). Facilitating professional ethical development: Beyond Kohlberg, Gilligan, Perry, & Fowler. *Proceedings of the Midwest Research-to-Practice Conference*. Columbus, OH.

English, L. M., & Gillen, M. A. (Eds.). (2001). *Promoting journal writing in adult education*. New Directions for Adult and Continuing Education (No. 90). San Francisco: Jossey-Bass.

Ermann, M. D. (Ed.). (1997). *Computers, ethics, and society* (2nd ed.). New York: Oxford University Press.

Etzioni, A. (1994). *The spirit of community: The reinvention of American society*. New York: Touchstone Books.

Etzioni, A. (1998). Moral dialogues: A communitarian core element. In A. L. Allen & M. C. Regan, Jr. (Eds.), *Debating democracy's discontent: Essays on American politics, law, and public philosophy* (pp. 183–192). Oxford: Oxford University Press.

Etzioni, A. (2000). Creating good communities and good societies. *Contemporary Sociology, 29*(1), 188–195.

Even, M. J. (1981). Adult educators should not necessarily be involved in social intervention. In B. W. Kreitlow & Associates, *Examining controversies in adult education* (pp. 40–44). San Francisco: Jossey-Bass.

Fagothey, A. (1972). *Right and reason: Ethics in theory and practice* (5th ed.). St. Louis: Mosby.

Flannery, D. D. (1993). [Review of *Self-direction in adult leaning: Perspectives on theory, research, and practice*]. *Adult Education Quarterly, 43*, 110–112.

Frankena, W. K. (1973). *Ethics* (2nd ed.). Englewood Cliffs, NJ: Prentice-Hall.

Gajdusek, L., & Gillotte, H. (1995). Teaching to the developmental needs of nonmainstream learners. In K. Taylor & C. Marienau (Eds.), *Learning environments for women's adult development: Bridges toward change* (pp. 45–52). New Directions for Adult and Continuing Education (No. 65). San Francisco: Jossey-Bass.

Galbraith, M. W. (Ed.). (1990). *Education through community organizations*. New Directions for Adult and Continuing Education (No. 47). San Francisco: Jossey-Bass.

Galbraith, M. W., Sisco, B. R., & Guglielmino, L. M. (1997). *Administering successful programs for adults*. Malabar, FL: Krieger.

Gibson, C. C., & Gibson, T. L. (1995). Lessons learned from 100+ years of distance learning. *Adult Learning, 7*(1), 15.

Gilligan, C. (1993). *In a different voice* (Reissued ed.). Cambridge, MA: Harvard University Press.

Gitomer, J. (1999). Negotiating strategies can make win-win situation. *Atlanta Business Chronicle*, August 9. Retrieved September 17, 2002, from http://atlanta.bcentral.com/atlanta/stories/1999/08/09/smallb3.html

Gordon, W., & Sork, T. J. (2001). Ethical issues and codes of ethics: Views of adult education practitioners in Canada and the United States. *Adult Education Quarterly, 51*, 202–218.

Grasha, A. F. (1994). A matter of style: The teacher as expert, formal authority, personal model, facilitator, and delegator. *College Teaching, 42*, 142–149.

Griffith, W. S. (1991). Do adult educators need a code of ethics? *Adult Learning, 2*(8), 1, 4.

Grill, J. (1999). Rethinking the promise of distance education. *Adult Learning, 10*(4), 32–33.

Guy, T. G. (Ed.). (1999). *Providing culturally relevant adult education: A challenge for the twenty-first century*. New Directions for Adult and Continuing Education (No. 82). San Francisco: Jossey-Bass.

Halberstam, J. (1993). *Everyday ethics: Inspired solutions to real-life dilemmas*. New York: Penguin.

Hammond, M., & Collins, R. (1991). *Self-directed learning: Critical practice*. New York: Nichols/GP Publishing.

Hansman, C. A., & Mott, V. W. (1999). Philosophy, dynamics and context: Program planning in action. *Adult Learning, 11*(2), 14–16.

Hartman, E. M. (1996). *Organizational ethics and the good life*. New York: Oxford University Press.

Hatcher, T. (2002). *Ethics and HRD*. Cambridge, MA: Perseus Publishing.

Hatcher, T., & Aragon, S. R. (2000a). A code of ethics and integrity for HRD research and practice. *Human Resource Development Quarterly, 11*(2), 179–185.

Hatcher, T., & Aragon, S. R. (2000b). Rationale for and development of a standard on ethics and integrity for international HRD research and practice. *Human Resource Development International, 3*(2), 207–219.

Hayes, E., & Colin, S. A. J., III. (Eds.). (1994). *Confronting racism and sexism*. New Directions for Adult and Continuing Education (No. 61). San Francisco: Jossey-Bass.

Healy, G. M. (1981). Adult educators should help citizens become involved in social reconstruction. In B. W. Kreitlow & Associates, *Examining controversies in adult education* (pp. 32–39). San Francisco: Jossey-Bass.

Heller, R. (1984). Blue collars and bluestockings: The Bryn Mawr Summer School for Women Workers, 1921–1938. In J. Kornbluh & M. Frederickson (Eds.), *Sisterhood and solidarity: Worker's education for women, 1914–1984* (pp. 107–145). Philadelphia: Temple University Press.

Hickman, C. J. (1999). Public policy implications associated with technology assisted distance education. *Adult Learning, 10*(3), 17–20.

Hiemstra, R. (1971). Witchcraft, black magic, and modern occultisms: An innovative adult education experience. *Adult Leadership, 20*(4), 147–148.

Hiemstra, R. (1988). Translating personal values and philosophy into practical action. In R. G. Brockett (Ed.), *Ethical issues in adult education* (pp. 178–194). New York: Teachers College Press.

Hiemstra, R. (Ed.). (1991). *Creating environments for effective adult learning.* New Directions for Adult and Continuing Education (No. 50). San Francisco: Jossey-Bass. Retrieved September 17, 2002, from http://www-distance.syr.edu/leindex.html

Hiemstra, R. (1994). Helping learners take responsibility for self-directed activities. In R. Hiemstra & R. G. Brockett (Eds.), *Overcoming resistance to self-direction in adult learning* (pp. 81–88). New Directions for Adult and Continuing Education (No. 64). San Francisco: Jossey-Bass. Retrieved September 17, 2002, from http://www-distance.syr.edu/ndacesdindex.html

Hiemstra, R. (1997). Applying the individualizing instruction model for adult learners. In C. R. Dills & A. J. Romiszowski (Eds.), *Instructional development paradigms* (pp. 555–570). Englewood Cliffs, NJ: Educational Technology Publications.

Hiemstra, R. (2000a). *The educative community: Linking the community, education, and family.* Baldwinsville, NY: HiTree Press. Retrieved September 17, 2002, from http://www-distance.syr.edu/commindx.html

Hiemstra, R. (2000b). Self-directed learning: The personal responsibility model. In G. A. Straka (Ed.), *Conceptions of self-directed learning* (pp. 93–108). Munster/New York: Waxmann.

Hiemstra, R. (2002a). *Lifelong learning: An exploration of adult and continuing education within a setting of lifelong learning needs.* Retrieved September 14, 2002, from http://www-distance.syr.edu/lll.html

Hiemstra, R. (2002b). *Roger Hiemstra's web page.* Retrieved March 25, 2003, from http://www-distance.syr.edu/

Hiemstra, R., & Brier, E. M. (1994). *Professional writing: Processes, strategies, and tips for publishing in educational journals*. Malabar, FL: Krieger.

Hiemstra, R., & Brockett, R. G. (1994). From behaviorism to humanism: Incorporating self-direction in learning concepts into the instructional design process. In H. B. Long & Associates, *New ideas about self-directed learning* (pp. 59–80). Norman, OK: Oklahoma Research Center for Continuing Professional and Higher Education, University of Oklahoma.

Hiemstra R., & Brockett, R. G. (1998). From mentor to partner: Lessons from a personal journey. In I. M. Saltiel, A. Sgori, & R. G. Brockett (Eds.), *The power and potential of collaborative learning partnerships* (pp. 43–52). New Directions for Adult and Continuing Education (No. 79). San Francisco: Jossey-Bass.

Hiemstra, R., & Long, R. (1974). A survey of 'felt' versus 'real' needs of physical therapists. *Adult Education, 24,* 270–279.

Hiemstra, R., & Sisco, B. R. (1990). *Individualizing instruction: Making learning personal, empowering, and successful.* San Francisco: Jossey-Bass. Retrieved September 12, 2002, from http://www-distance.syr.edu/iiindex.html

Holt, M. E. (1998). Ethical considerations in internet-based adult education. In B. Cahoon (Ed.), *Adult learning and the internet* (pp. 63–70). New Directions for Adult and Continuing Education (No. 78). San Francisco: Jossey-Bass.

Hopey, C. E., & Ginsburg, L. (1996). Distance learning and new technologies. *Adult Learning, 8*(1), 22–23.

Horton, M., Kohl, J., & Kohl, H. (1990). *The long haul: An autobiography.* New York: Doubleday.

Houle, C. O. (1961). *The inquiring mind.* Madison, WI: The University of Wisconsin Press.

Houle, C. O. (1980). *Continuing learning in the professions.* San Francisco: Jossey-Bass.

House, E. R. (1996a). Ethical considerations for evaluators and researchers. In C. MacNeil & K. Maxwell (Eds.), *Proceedings of the 1996 Edward F. Kelly Evaluation Conference* (pp. 29–35). Albany, NY: The Evaluation Consortium at Albany, School of Education, University at Albany, State University of New York.

House, E. R. (1996b). Evaluation in the marketplace. In C. MacNeil & K. Maxwell (Eds.), *Proceedings of the 1996 Edward F. Kelly Evaluation Conference* (pp. 14–17). Albany, NY: The Evaluation Consortium at Albany, School of Education, University of Albany, State University of New York.

House, V. W. (1990). Let the people choose. *Adult Learning, 2*(3), 14, 16–17.

Huber, N. S. (1997). Effective administrators are managers and leaders. *Adult Learning, 9*(1), 10–11, 30.

Hunter, J. (1991). *Culture wars: The struggle to define America.* New York: BasicBooks.

Hunter, J. (1994). *Before the shooting begins: Searching for democracy in America's culture war.* New York: The Free Press.

Hyman, M. (1996). *MKTG 550: Business/marketing ethics.* Retrieved September 14, 2002, from http://cbae.nmsu.edu/~mktgwww/hyman/m550syl.htm

Ilsley, P. J. (1992). The undeniable link: Adult and continuing education and social change. In M. W. Galbraith & B. R. Sisco (Eds.), *Confronting controversies in challenging times: A call for action* (pp. 25–34). New Directions for Adult and Continuing Education (No. 54). San Francisco: Jossey-Bass.

Imel, S. (1995). *Inclusive adult learning environments* (ERIC Digest No. 162). Retrieved September 17, 2002, from http://www.ed.gov/databases/ERIC_Digests/ed385779.html

James, W. B. (1992). Professional certification is not needed in adult and continuing education. In M. W. Galbraith & B. R. Sisco, (Eds.), *Confronting controversies in challenging times: A call for action* (pp. 125–131). New Directions for Adult and Continuing Education (No. 54). San Francisco: Jossey-Bass.

Jarvis, P. (1997). *Ethics and education for adults in a late modern society.* Leicester, UK: National Institute of Adult Continuing Education (England and Wales).

Johnson, D. G. (2000). *Computer ethics* (3rd ed.). Upper Saddle River, NJ: Prentice-Hall.

Johnson, D. G., & Nissenbaum, H. (Eds.). (1995). *Computers, ethics, and social values.* Upper Saddle River, NJ: Prentice-Hall.

Jones, A., Scanlon, E., & Blake, C. (2000). Conferencing in communities of learners: Examples from social history and science communication. *Educational Technology & Society, 3*(3). Retrieved September 12, 2002, from http://ifets.ieee.org/periodical/vol_3_2000/c02.html

Kasworm, C. E. (1988). Facilitating ethical development: A paradox. In R. G. Brockett (Ed.), *Ethical issues in adult education* (pp. 17–33). New York: Teachers College Press.

Kasworm, C. E. (1992). Adult learners in academic settings: Self-directed learning within the formal learning context. In H. B. Long

& Associates, *Self-directed learning: Application and research* (pp. 223–244). Norman, OK: Oklahoma Research Center for Continuing Professional and Higher Education, University of Oklahoma.

Keller, J. (1998). Moral dialogue within the ethics consultation: Possibilities and pitfalls. *Contexts, 7*(1). Retrieved September 17, 2002, from http://www.uhmc.sunysb.edu/prevmed/mns/imcs/contexts/blair/jean.html

Keyes, R. F. (2002). *Marketing ethics and creative thinking.* Retrieved September 14, 2002, from http://www.swcollege.com/marketing/gitm/gitm09-5.html

Kidder, R. M. (1994). *Shared values for a troubled world: Conversations with men and women of conscience.* San Francisco: Jossey-Bass.

Kidder, R. M. (1995). *How good people make tough choices: Resolving the dilemmas of ethical living.* New York: Fireside.

Knowles, M. S. (1980). *The modern practice of adult education: From pedogogy to andragogy* (Revised and updated). Chicago: Association Press.

Knowles, M. S. (1986). *Using learning contracts.* San Francisco: Jossey-Bass.

Knox, A. B. (1962). *The audience for liberal adult education.* Chicago: Center for the Study of Liberal Education for Adults.

Kogut, B. (2002). *News and events.* Syracuse, NY: Laubach Literacy. Retrieved September 18, 2002, from http://www.laubach.org/NEWS/indexnews.html

Kohlberg, L. (1981). *Essays on moral development: Vol. 1. The philosophy of moral development: Moral states and the idea of justice.* San Francisco: Harper & Row.

Kornbluh, J., & Frederickson, M. (1984). *Sisterhood and solidarity: Workers education for women, 1914–1984.* Philadelphia: Temple University Press.

Krathwohl, D. R., Bloom, B. S., & Masia, B. B. (1964). *Taxonomy of educational objectives: The classification of educational goals: Handbook II. Affective domain.* New York: McKay.

Laubach Literacy Action. (1996). *National quality standards for volunteer literacy programs.* Syracuse, NY: Author.

Lawler, P. A. (1996). Ethics, equity, and hidden privilege. *Adult Learning, 8*(2), 18–19.

Lawler, P. A. (2000). The ACHE code of ethics: Its role for the profession. *Journal of Continuing Higher Education, 48*(3), 31–34.

Lawler, P. A., & Fielder, J. H. (1991). Analyzing ethical problems in continuing higher education: A model for practical use. *Journal of Continuing Higher Education, 39*(2), 20–24.

Lawler, P. A., & King, K. P. (2000). *Planning for effective faculty development.* Malabar, FL: Krieger.

Lewis, H. (2000). *A question of values: Six ways we make the personal choices that shape our lives* (Revised and updated edition). Crozet, VA: Axios Press.

Lindeman, E. C. (1989). *The meaning of adult education.* Norman, OK: Oklahoma Research Center for Continuing Professional and Higher Education, University of Oklahoma. (Original work published in 1926).

Long, H. B., & Associates. (2000). *Self-directed learning and the information age* (available only as an interactive CD-ROM. For information contact Motorola University, 1500 Gateway Boulevard, MS 93, Boynton Beach, FL 33426–8292). Ordering information retrieved September 14, 2002, from http://sdlglobal.com/2000_publication_intro.html

Lovell, M. G. (1993). Technology: How is it used in programs? *Adult Learning, 4*(3), 32–33.

MacKinnon, B. (2001). *Ethics: Theory and contemporary issues* (3rd ed.). Belmont, CA: Wadsworth/Thompson Learning.

Marsh, D. (1991). *50 ways to fight censorship: And important facts to know about the censors.* New York: Thunder's Mouth Press.

Massey, D. (1992). A place called home? *New Formations, 17*(Summer), 3–15.

McCrickerd, J. (n.d.). *Technology and ethics.* Retrieved September 14, 2002, from http://www.drake.edu/artsci/philrel/fachomepages/jenhomepage/Technology@Ethics.html

McDonald, K. S., & Wood, G. S., Jr. (1993). Surveying adult education practitioners about ethical issues. *Adult Education Quarterly, 43,* 243–257.

Merriam, S. B., & Brockett, R. G. (1997). *The profession and practice of adult education: An introduction.* San Francisco: Jossey-Bass.

Mezirow, J. (1984). [Review of the report of the CCEU Project to develop standards and criteria for good practice in continuing education *Principles of good practice in continuing education*]. *Lifelong Learning: An Omnibus of Practice and Research, 8*(3), 27–28, 30.

Mirvits, P. H., & Seashore, S. E. (1979). Being ethical in organizational research. *American Psychologist, 34,* 766–780.

Mitcham, C. (Ed.). (2000). *Research in philosophy and technology: Metaphysics, epistemology, and technology* (Vol. 19). Greenwich, CT: JAI Press.

Mitcham, C. (2001a). *Political ethics and technology*. Retrieved September 14, 2002, from http://www.egs.edu/faculty/carlmitcham.html

Mitcham, C. (2001b). *Technological reflection on campus*. Lanham, MD: Rowman & Littlefield Publishers, Inc.

Moe, J. F. (1990). Education, democracy, and cultural pluralism: Continuing higher education in an age of diversity. In J. M. Ross-Gordon, L. G. Martin, & D. B. Briscoe (Eds.), *Serving culturally diverse populations* (pp. 31–44). New Directions for Adult and Continuing Education (No. 48). San Francisco: Jossey-Bass.

Morgan, P. W., & Reynolds, G. H. (1997). *The appearance of impropriety*. New York: Free Press.

National Coalition Against Censorship. (n.d.). *Free expression after September 11th*. Retrieved September 12, 2002, from http://www.ncac.org/issues/freeex911.html

Nelms, K. R. (1993). Information technologies and self-directed learning: Structures for evaluation and application. In H. B. Long & Associates, *Emerging perspectives of self-directed learning* (pp. 141–160). Norman, OK: Oklahoma Research Center for Continuing Professional and Higher Education, University of Oklahoma.

Pearson, E. M., & Podeschi, R. L. (1999). Humanism and individualism: Maslow and his critics. *Adult Education Quarterly, 50*, 41–55.

People for the American Way. (2002). *People for the American way*. Retrieved September 13, 2002, from http://www.pfaw.org/

Peters, J. M. (1991). Strategies for reflective practice. In R. G. Brockett (Ed.), *Professional development for educators of adults* (pp. 89–96). New Directions for Adult and Continuing Education (No. 51). San Francisco: Jossey-Bass.

Peters, J. M., & Armstrong, J. L. (1998). Collaborative learning: People laboring together to construct knowledge. In I. M. Saltiel, A. Sgroi, & R. G. Brockett (Eds.), *The power and potential of collaborative learning partnerships* (pp. 75–85). New Directions for Adult and Continuing Education (No. 79). San Francisco: Jossey-Bass.

Peters, J. M., Jarvis, P., & Associates. (1991). *Adult education: Evolution and achievements in a developing field of study*. San Francisco: Jossey-Bass.

Piskurich, G. M. (1992). Preparing the learner for self-directed learning. In H. B. Long & Associates, *Self-directed learning: Application and research* (pp. 309–322). Norman, OK: Oklahoma Research Center for Continuing Professional and Higher Education, University of Oklahoma.

Pojman, L. P. (1995). *Ethics: Discovering right and wrong* (2nd ed.). Belmont, CA: Wadsworth.

Pojman, L. P. (2001). *Ethics: Discovering right and wrong* (4th ed.). Belmont, CA: Wadsworth.

Preston, I. L. (1996). *The great American blow-up: Puffery in advertising and selling.* Madison, WI: University of Wisconsin Press.

Price, D. W. (1997). Ethical dilemmas in administrative practice. *Adult Learning, 9*(1), 15–17.

Progoff, I. (1992). *At a journal workshop: Writing to access the power of the unconscious and evoke creative ability* (Rev. ed.). Los Angeles: J. P. Tarcher.

Purtill, R. L. (1976). *Thinking about ethics.* Englewood Cliffs, NJ: Prentice-Hall.

Purtilo, R. B., & Cassel, C. K. (1981). *Ethical dimensions in the health professions.* Philadelphia: Saunders.

Putnam, R. D. (2000). *Bowling alone: The collapse and revival of American community.* New York: Simon & Schuster.

Raths, L. E., Harmin, M., & Simon, S. B. (1975). Values and valuing. In D. A. Reed & S. B. Simon (Eds.), *Humanistic education sourcebook* (pp. 72–81). Englewood Cliffs, NJ: Prentice-Hall.

Reinsmith, W. A. (1994). Archetypal forms in teaching. *College Teaching, 42,* 131–136.

Rogers, C. R. (1961). *On becoming a person.* Boston: Houghton-Mifflin.

Rose, A. (1993). Technology—Servant or master? *Adult Learning, 4*(3), 6, 30.

Rosen, H. (2000). Bush puts faith in a social service role. *Washington Post,* May 5, A01.

Ross, K. L. (1999). *Rights, responsibilities, and communitarianism.* Retrieved September 17, 2002, from http://www.friesian.com/rights.htm

Ross-Gordon, J. M. (1993). Multicultural issues in adult education: Where we've come from, where we are now, where we're going. *PAACE Journal of Lifelong Learning, 2,* 43–56.

Schwartz, D. J. (1965). *The magic of thinking big.* Englewood Cliffs, NJ: Prentice-Hall.

Scriven, M. (1982). Professional ethics. *Journal of Higher Education, 53,* 307–317.

Sheared, V., & Sissel, P. A. (Ed.). (2001). *Making space: Merging theory and practice in adult education.* Westport, CT: Bergin & Garvey.

Shrader-Frechette, K., & Westra, L. (1997). *Technology and values.* Lanham, MD: Rowman & Littlefield Publishers, Inc.

Siegel, I. H. (2000). Toward developing a universal code of ethics for adult educators. *PAACE Journal of Lifelong Learning, 9,* 39–64.

Simon, S. B. (1993). *In search of values: 31 strategies for finding out what really matters most to you.* New York: Warner Books.

Simon, S. B., Howe, L. W., & Kirschenbaum, H. (1978). *Values clarification: A handbook of practical strategies for teachers and students* (Rev. ed.). New York: Hart.

Singarella, T. A., & Sork, T. J. (1983). Questions of values and conduct: Ethical issues for educators of adults. *Adult Education Quarterly, 33,* 244–251.

Singer, P. (2000). *Writings on an ethical life.* New York: HarperCollins.

Sisco, B. (1997). The individualizing instruction model for adult learners. In C. R. Dills & A. J. Romiszowski (Eds.), *Instructional development paradigms* (pp. 391–400). Englewood Cliffs, NJ: Educational Technology Publications.

Sisco, B. R. (1988). Dilemmas in continuing education administration. In R. G. Brockett (Ed.), *Ethical issues in adult education* (pp. 64–87). New York: Teachers College Press.

Skinner, B. F. (1954). The science of learning and the art of teaching. *Harvard Educational Review, 24*(2), 86–97.

Software Publishers Association. (2002). *Software piracy: Is it happening in your school or university?* Retrieved September 14, 2002, from http://www.thejournal.com/magazine/vault/A1984.cfm

Solomon, R. C. (1992). *Ethics and excellence: Cooperation and integrity in business.* New York: Oxford University Press.

Sork, T. J. (1988). Ethical issues in program planning. In R. G. Brockett (Ed.), *Ethical issues in adult education* (pp. 34–50). New York: Teachers College Press.

Sork, T. J. (1990, October). *An "ethical practices analysis" for adult educators.* Paper presented at the annual American Association for Adult and Continuing Education conference, Salt Lake City, UT.

Sork, T. J. (1997). Workshop planning. In J. A. Fleming (Ed.), *New perspectives on designing and implementing effective workshops* (pp. 5–18). New Directions for Adult and Continuing Education (No. 76). San Francisco: Jossey-Bass.

Sork, T. J., & Welock, B. A. (1992). Adult and continuing education needs a code of ethics. In M. W. Galbraith & B. R. Sisco (Eds.),

Confronting controversies in challenging times: A call for action (pp. 115–122). New Directions for Adult and Continuing Education (No. 54). San Francisco: Jossey-Bass.

Stalker, J. (2001). Misogyny, women, and obstacles in tertiary education: A vile situation. *Adult Education Quarterly, 51,* 288–305.

Steinman, S. O., Richardson, N. F., & McEnroe, T. (1998). *The ethical decision-making manual for helping professionals.* Pacific Grove, CA: Brooks/Cole.

Stewart, D. W. (1987). *Adult learning in America: Eduard Lindeman and his agenda for lifelong learning.* Malabar, FL: Krieger.

Taylor, K., & Marienau, C. (Eds.). (1995). *Learning environments for women's adult development: Bridges toward change.* New Directions for Adult and Continuing Education (No. 65). San Francisco: Jossey-Bass.

Thiroux, J. P. (1986). *Ethics: Theory and practice* (3rd ed.). New York: Macmillan.

Thompson, M. (2000). *Teach yourself ethics.* Lincolnwood, IL: NTC Publishing Group.

Tisdell, E. (1993). Feminism and adult learning: Power, pedagogy and praxis. In S. B. Merriam (Ed.), *An update on adult learning theory* (pp. 91–104). New Directions for Adult and Continuing Education (No. 57). San Francisco: Jossey-Bass.

Tisdell, E. J., & Taylor, E. W. (1999). Adult education philosophy informs practice. *Adult Learning, 11*(2), 6–10.

Tough, A. (1979). *The adult's learning projects: A fresh approach to theory and practice in adult learning* (2nd ed.). Austin, TX: Learning Concepts. (Original work published in 1971).

Tyler, R. (1974). *Basic principles of curriculum and instruction.* Chicago: University of Chicago Press.

University of Southern Mississippi. (2000). *Educational leadership in information policy and ethics.* Retrieved September 12, 2002, from http://www.lib.usm.edu/~mla/publications/ml/winter00/slis.html

Velázquez, L. C. (1993). *Migrant adult perceptions of schooling, learning, and education.* Unpublished doctoral dissertation, University of Tennessee, Knoxville.

Warwick, D. P., & Kelman, H. C. (1976). Ethical issues in social intervention. In W. G. Bennis, K. D. Benne, & R. Chin (Eds.), *The planning of change* (3rd ed., pp. 470–496). New York: Holt, Rinehart, & Winston.

Weston, A. (1997). *A practical companion to ethics.* New York and Oxford: Oxford University Press.

Willing, D. C., Morford, J., & Haney, H. (1998). Where to draw the line: Ten tips for maintaining proper professional boundaries with adult students. *Professional Tips for Adult and Continuing Educators*, 6(1), Published by the American Association for Adult and Continuing Education, Washington, DC.

Wilson, A. L., & Cervero, R. M. (1996). Who sits at the planning table: Ethics and planning practice. *Adult Learning*, 8(2), 20–22.

Wilson, E. O. (1998). *Consilience: The unity of knowledge*. New York: Alfred A. Knopf.

Wilson, K. E. (1982). Power, pretense, piggybacking: Some ethical issues in teaching. *Journal of Higher Education*, 53, 268–281.

Wood, G. S., Jr. (1996). A code of ethics for all adult educators? *Adult Learning*, 8(2), 13–14.

Zinn, L. M. (1990). Identifying your personal orientation. In M. W. Galbraith (Ed.), *Adult learning methods* (pp. 39–77). Malabar, FL: Krieger.

Zinn, L. M. (1993). Do the right thing: Ethical decision making in professional and business practice. *Adult Learning*, 5(2), 7–8.

INDEX

Academy of Human Resource
     Development, 90
Association for Continuing
     Higher Education, 9,
     89–90

Behaviorism, 126
Beliefs about human nature,
     19–20
Bryn Mawr summer school for
     women workers, 53

Censorship. *See* Ethical
     dilemmas
Certification of professional
     educators, 94
Code of ethics, 9–10, 87–88
Codifying ethical practice,
     88–91
Commission of Professors of
     Adult Education, 89
Communitarianism, 99
Community, 99–101
Computer Ethics Institute, 57
Conflicting obligations, 27–28
Conflicting responsibilities,
     26–27
Consequential theories, 21
Continuing education and
     profit, 50–51
Critical reflection, 117

Deontological theories, 21
Descriptive ethics, 5
Dimensions of ethical practice,
     14–15

Ethical concerns, 1
Ethical decision making, 15, 24
     and critical reflection, 16
     questions as guide to, 17,
          66–68
Ethical decision making (EDM)
     model, 15–31, 70
     consequences, 15, 28–31
     illustration, 16
     obligations, 15, 26–28
     responsibility, 26
     values, 15, 17–25, 60
     worksheet, 72–74, 85
Ethical dilemmas, 4, 10, 52
     advocacy for social change,
          53–55
     censorship, 57, 59–61
     marketing, 62–63, 64
     right versus right, 13, 27,
          105
     right versus wrong, 13
     self-directed learning, 63, 65–
          66, 67
     in teaching, 36–37, 40–45
     technology, 56–57, 58–59
     and the World Wide Web, 56

Ethical environment, 98
  creation of, 98, 101–103
  specific strategies, 108–111
Ethical practice, 1
  dimensions of, 14–15
  guidelines, 94–97
  nonconfrontational approach,
    103–105
Ethical Practices Analysis, 110
Ethical questions
  in planning programs, 39
  in teaching or training
    adults, 38
Ethical relativism, 95
Ethical research questions,
  118–120
Ethical standards, 87
Ethics
  and adult education, 7, 19
  defined, 4–5
  and human nature, 19
  human resource development, 9
  and justice, 25
  and moral development, 114
  and morality, 5
  and moral obligation, 19
  and multiple responsibilities,
    14–15
  and philosophical beliefs,
    115–116
  philosophy, 9
  professional power, 2, 3
  and program planning, 10,
    45–51
  and research, 118–120
  and respect, 25
  and training, 7

Highlander Research and Education Center, 53
Hull-House, 53

Humanism, 102, 126
  humanistic orientation, 102
  humanistic thought, 19
Human resource development,
  9, 11

Idealism, 124
Inclusivity, 104
International Self-Directed
    Learning Symposium,
    63, 65
Involving learners in the plan-
    ning process, 46–47

Keeping a professional distance,
    41–44

Laubach Literacy, 89
Liberalism, 125
Literacy Volunteers of
    America, 89

Marketing. *See* Ethical dilemmas
Metaethics, 6
Model for ethical decision mak-
    ing. *See* Ethical decision
    making model
Modeling ethical behavior, 118

Nonconfrontational approach
    to ethical practice, 103–105
Nonconsequential theories, 21
Normative ethics, 6

Personal beliefs, 18, 20
Personal code of ethics, 111
Personal philosophy of educa-
    tion, 20, 35
  personal philosophy state-
    ment, 9, 35–36, 121–123
  worksheet, 128

Personal responsibility, 107–108
Personal values, 20, 60
Philosophical systems, 123
Philosophy of adult education
    inventory, 122
Professional writing, 117
Progressivism, 102, 125
ProLiteracy Worldwide, 89

Radicalism, 127
Realism, 124
Research. *See* Ethical research
Resolving conflicts, 109
Responding to ethical dilem-
    mas, 77, 79–84. *See also*
    Ethical dilemmas
  accepting a situation, 80
  leaving an organization, 84
  overlooking behaviors, 79–80
  persuading others, 81
  subverting policies, 81–82
  whistle-blowing, 82–83
Responding to perceived needs, 48
Response-able, 34
Right versus right, 13, 27, 105
Right versus wrong, 13

Self-directed learning. *See* Ethi-
    cal dilemmas
Self-improvement, 116–117
Social change. *See* Ethical
    dilemmas

Standards for graduate pro-
    grams in adult educa-
    tion, 89
Staying current on changing
    information, 44–45

Teacher as expert or facilita-
    tor, 37
Technology. *See* Ethical dilemmas
Teleological theories, 21
Third party involvement, 111

Universal code of ethics.
    See Code of ethics

Values, 23
  acceptance, 23
  commitment, 23
  preference, 23
  shared, 109
Values clarification, 18

Watergate, 1
Whistle-blowing, 82–83
Win-win situation, 106
Withholding information, 49
Workshop on creating a state-
    ment of personal philoso-
    phy, 121–123
World Wide Web, 56, 117